NOTES
to my
SON

From Being a Boy to Becoming a Good and Successful Man

DAVID A. DIXON

Notes to My Son © *2015 by David A. Dixon*

ISBN 978-0-9827798-3-5

First Edition, 2015

Cover and Layout design by The Dixon Group, Inc.

Published by The Dixon Group, Inc.

Published in the United States of America

For more information on this and other titles by David A. Dixon, Visit:
www.davidadixon.net

Acknowledgements

First, I give thanks to God for blessing me with the wisdom to write this book. I give thanks to family and friends too numerous to mention, but you know who you are.

I give many thanks to my wife, Jada, for her support, love, and coming into my life and just plain "getting me." I love you with all of my soul. Thank you for the gift of another daughter, Maia Galan. What a difference you both make in my life. Many thanks to my new sister-in-law, mother-in-law and her husband; Joy Roberts, Sandra "Coco" Roberts-Taylor, and Tracy Taylor. I love you all and I'm so happy we've become a family.

I'd like to thank my children, Brandon, Kenadi, and Daniel, for giving me the inspiration to write this book. Thanks to my parents, Leona and Carl Dixon, my brother and his family; Dean, Darlyne, Jaseri, Jaslynn and Jalel Dixon. My sisters Toni Bridges, Tamie Smith, and Terri Gentry as well as my Brother-in-law, Dwight Gentry.

Many thanks to my close friends who have been the father's I've looked up to, learned from, and asked for of advice. They are; Thomas Townsend, Darryl Lucas, Calvin London, Tony Brooks, Odell Stroud, Rudy Murray, Anthony Marshall and Richard Weddle. Whenever I think of exemplary fathers, I start with you gentlemen. You guys have provided me with some incredible insight, and I can't tell you enough how much I've appreciated it and how valuable it's been! Also much love and thanks to Marc Alford and Trentn Walker, who've shared some of their parenting insights with me.

In addition, I can't leave out some mothers and women who I've also leaned on for advice, direction and encouragement. They are Demeeta Hulett, Corliss Whatley, Dr. Rosalyn Pitts, Julia Bell, Paula Martin, Dr. Paula Gallegos, Carolyn McKenzie and Kathy Stroud. You've been awesome friends, and a guy couldn't ask for better.

Much thanks goes to Devaughn Bowens and Terrance Weathersby, as well as many other students, too numerous to mention, for their input. I appreciate you.

Shout out to students at East High School and George Washington High School in Denver, Colorado! Thanks also to some of their teachers who always have me speak with their classes; Tamara Rhone, Wherda Utsey, and Unity Hartman, respectively.

Since this book is about being a father, I would be remiss if I didn't acknowledge some other great fathers I grew up with. Thanks, Vern Harris, Wayne Vaden, Pastor Robert E. Martin, Jr., Phil Strickland, Tim Alford, and Marvin Marshall, to name a few.

Thanks to my Editor, Traci Jones, who has been a God send and completely annoying, yet very on point! Man, I don't know what I'd do without your insight, constant questioning and a great eye for catching all the little things that make a difference. You're a gem!

I also must give thanks to the guidance I've received from my Uncles, Napoleon and Lonnie Fuller, my grandmother, Irene Riley, my Aunts, Sadie Ashby, and Mable Fuller. Also thanks to Dr. Peggy Norwood and Dr. Jerry Anderson for their friendship, support, and very informative input about raising children. I love you all.

Thank you, Simon Tang, for helping out with the cover design and Alan Lavizzo for the kind review!

This book is dedicated to my son, Brandon.

Table of Contents

Foreword

Being a father is difficult, and yet Dixon takes on this task, as well as associated conversations, head-on and does not shy away from the tough topics. He speaks as a mentor, tutor, coach, and father in *Notes to My Son*. Dixon does not mince words; his straightforward, unapologetic honesty is what endears the reader to the conversation.

Dixon has written this narrative, the story of life, in a way that encourages participation. He guides young men toward becoming (or being) grown men. He writes this book out of love for his children and for all young men, but especially for those who may not have a father figure in their life.

Every young man should read this book. It will resonate with them, and perhaps change the way they see themselves. As with all books that are labors of love, this book can be a game-changer.

Dixon is part of the new wave of untraditional authors. This book gives voice to the fathers of color who have traditionally not been heard. Dixon grew up in urban settings and did not always have the guidance he desired as a young man. Rather than being resentful, he chooses to share his wisdom, not only with his sons, but with all sons.

~ Paula Gallegos, Ph.D.

Paula has taught English and college social science courses in urban public secondary schools for over 15 years, most recently in Denver Public Schools. She earned her Ph.D. in Educational Leadership and Innovation from the University of Colorado Denver where her research focuses on academic achievement in high school for underserved students from urban public schools. She has also recently contributed to two publications: Confronting Racism in Higher Education, and the Encyclopedia of Diversity and Social Justice. Currently, Paula is the undergraduate residency coordinator for the NxtGEN program at the University of Colorado Denver. The NxtGEN program is designed to recruit, support, and train urban youth to go into teaching so they can graduate college, teach, and diversify the teacher workforce in urban communities in hopes of improving academic and life outcomes for the next generation of urban youth.

Author's Note

This book was started on September 21, 2006 because I knew my son would want his book on his thirteenth birthday since I was going to give his older sister one on hers.

Sure enough, after giving my daughter a book on her thirteenth birthday, before she could even put her hands on it, my son was mad and asking where his book was? Well, for starters, it wasn't his birthday. But secondly, even though I pondered it over for years, I wasn't as comfortable writing a book for him as I was for my daughter. This book took substantially longer because I know from experience becoming a good man is hard work.

Nevertheless, I pulled myself together and began to write for him. Here are some lessons to help him learn and grow as a young man. Hopefully, this will help him avoid many of the pitfalls in life as well. Just as hopefully, whether you are reading this for yourself or giving it to your son or a friend, I hope it adds the same value.

These "lessons' are what I've learned growing up as a young man and as an adult. Now, to the work!

A Note for My Son

Dearest Brandon,

As a father, I've struggled with how much affection I should demonstrate toward you. Don't misunderstand this, I love you dearly. It's just that internally, I've had issues with figuring out how to make you hard enough to stand up to cruelness, difficult circumstances, and bullies. At the same time, I've wanted to make you soft enough to be a caring, sympathetic, and loving human being.

I think many dads struggle with this same thing and that is why some are so hardcore with their sons. We can forget the importance of the need to be kind and gentle fathers, so our children have a loving core. For it is your core upon which you will build your foundation of power, principles, and protection. I want you to be strong, not picked on, because being picked on hurt me so much when I was young. I want you to be able to fight and protect yourself, should the need occur. I'd even like you to be so skilled and powerful that you have the ability only to give bullies a look, and they would decide they don't even want to try you.

I want you to be tough and yet I've been unsure of how to help get you there. Don't get me wrong, I already think you are tough in a number of ways and playing sports has certainly helped with that. When I say tough, I'm not just talking about fighting. I'm talking about three-hundred-and-sixty-degree toughness, which includes mental, spiritual, emotional and physical toughness. I want people to like you, but not be able to take advantage of you. I want you to feel comfortable around anyone, regardless of whether they are a thug or a CEO. I also want you to be gentle at the right times and have that loving, nurturing touch that is necessary for life. It is something that people respect and admire. It is like a super power everyone can see, hear and feel, but the balance between toughness and gentleness is difficult to achieve.

I struggle with what all parents struggle with; how to protect my children. Watching you grow has been amazing. To think this baby I used to carry around on my shoulders when I was mowing the lawn is now this teenage kid that can take me to the hoop when we play basketball is amazing!

What I don't want is for you to experience many of the pains I have had to suffer. For example, I experienced significant teasing and bullying early on. I also was such a jerk at one point during my sophomore year in high school that a considerable number of girls were mad at me for a few weeks. I don't want you to have to go through any of that. But if you do, despite my wishes, I feel my job is to equip you with ways to make better choices. Doing so should help you avoid having some of my experiences or at least allow you to handle them better than I did if they do occur. Of course, you can choose to be smarter than me and not do some of the things I did that contributed to putting me in bad situations in the first place.

As a father, I've been unsure of how to write a prescription that helps you turn out to be tough and loving, all wrapped up in one. What I do know is throughout all of my parenting, I've wanted to raise you to be a good man who loves, respects others, and is comfortable with who he is as a person. Finding out "who" you are is a journey, just like becoming a man is.

One thing I am proud of in watching you grow is seeing that you've already figured out some of these things and you've helped teach me how to become a better parent. I've learned a great deal from watching you, Daniel, and your sister grow and by just interacting with you. I can never truly express how grateful I am for having this opportunity.

Now, on to some subjects I hope will help you be a good man, if not a great one. I hope they will add value to your life, help protect you, and at times be a flashlight that can guide you out of darkness. I hope you will be able to re-read this book as you get older and continue to find value.

When it gets right down to it, *Notes to My Daughter* was a love letter to your sister. This book, my son, is a love letter to you. The following are things I want you to understand, learn more about, and also avoid.

All My Love,
Dad

Lesson 1.

Trust God

The importance of faith in your life

"If you don't believe in God but are more a fan of evolution or the Big Bang Theory, I have four questions? First, who said, "Bang?" Second, how did all of that stuff that went bang get here? Further, how did it get here in such a manner that it could combine itself to create something? Easy, the laws of physics. And who made these laws? Yes, the Almighty God."

~ David Dixon

I have put this first in your book as well as your sister's because I believe so strongly that both young men and women need to have a strong sense of faith. I don't know where I'd be had it not been for my faith. When I've had big challenges and great sadness in my life, my faith is the only thing that got me through them.

Before and after becoming a father, I had several tough times; some of which drove me into severe states of depression. What kept me going was my faith, my hope, and knowing that if I were not here to guide you, I'd be leaving you in the hands of someone else. Without faith in God, along with hope, I believe we all would have nothing, and at times, I would have felt like I had no reason to live.

Faith and hope that somehow I'd make it through, are the only things that kept me going when I've lost a job or loved one. They are the only things that kept me going when I've failed a test, or broken up with a girlfriend. It's weird how He makes that work, but He does.

When I've had bad things happen, or tragedies occur, I've been consumed with them. Literally, every single minute of the day, thoughts about that situation or person would replay in my mind. This made things worse. I've gone to sleep and dreamt about it all night; which was totally annoying, frustrating, and excruciatingly painful. Especially, when I knew I was going to spend the rest of the next day thinking about it all over again.

In my darkest hours of life, I've made a choice to believe that things would get better. I've held on to faith and hope that some way, somehow, things would get better. I feel this is the only reason I'm still here, and it may be the only reason many others are as well.

You will need to develop and nourish your spirituality. I've witnessed miracles in my life and in others. As for people who don't believe in miracles, they should think about all of the diseases they don't have. They should think about all of the drunk drivers they've seen or haven't seen, yet passed by successfully and lived. They should think about the number of stop lights they've driven through during their lives and either have not been hit by someone running one of them or survived it if they were hit. They should think about all of the people with mental health issues and who possess a propensity for violence that they've been around and yet, have not been hurt or killed. It's a miracle any one of us lives a long time.

My point is that life, as well as the quality of one's life, isn't a given; it's a blessing. I don't believe we should live our lives without thought or faith.

Lesson 2.

Becoming A Real Man

Taking care of yourself and your responsibilities

"Go Away Little Boy" ~ title of a song by Marlena Shaw

GROWN BOYS vs. GROWN MEN

So many boys and young men in today's world grow up to be nothing but bigger boys. Too many of today's men are imposters. They look like men, but they act like boys. That's not what I want for you and I certainly hope you don't want that for yourself. There are few things worse than seeing grown men acting like little boys, throwing temper tantrums, wearing sagging pants, being financially irresponsible, or not taking care of their children. Many can't even take care of themselves and depend on their parents, women, or others to do it for them. When I was growing up, real men didn't depend on others to take care of them. They took care of themselves. They were raised to do so and it was expected.

My idea of fulfilling your duties as a man isn't becoming one and still conducting yourself like a little boy. Nor is it being taken care of by the prison system. This isn't to say every man in prison is there because he didn't grow up to be a man. What I am saying is many made decisions that allowed them to get caught up in the judicial system, ending in imprisonment. Others got in situations where the judicial system abused them. Although, from my view, there **are** a number of men who are in prison because they never bought into taking care of themselves, or they became content with just letting the system do it. I have more respect for a man working in a low wage position, paying his own bills, working his way up, than I do for a man who has someone else paying his way.

Sometimes, when you put a working man next to a man who is taken care of, you can't tell the difference. The one who's taken care of may even be better dressed and have a nicer car. Despite this, there is a staggering difference between the two! For example, someone else may have bought those clothes or car for the first guy. For this reason, when a woman looks at both, side by side, on one hand she sees the real deal but on the other, what she's actually seeing is an illusion.

Please understand this; real women will not be interested in taking care of any grown man and a real man won't allow it, at least not for very long. Remember that. There are a number of unrealistic, juvenile, and emotionally immature young ladies and women who are okay with taking care of men. Nevertheless, real women want independent, strong, self-assured men who are capable of providing for themselves.

Son, this is why I'm raising you the way I am. I want you to learn the difference between being a boy and being a man. I want you to understand the importance of using skills you've learned as a child and as a teenager, and the knowledge shared by other men, to make your own way in life. Put your life in your hands and manage it, don't leave it up to someone else.

Being a man can be difficult and challenging. But, I firmly believe that being a man starts with having or developing very specific character traits. Real men are: giving, loving, firm yet flexible, good listeners, compassionate, emotionally healthy, and mentally sharp. Real men do: take care of their children's emotional and financial needs, take care of their parents, and help their families. Real men aren't: liars, moochers, thieves, schemers, drug dealers, pimps, crybabies, losers, obnoxious or greedy. Real men don't: abuse women, disrespect others, think only of themselves, avoid responsibilities, financially depend on others, or treat others with uncaring, ruthless attitudes.

Real men are respected by their families and perhaps by the public. Their actions reflect their words and consistently show they respect themselves. You cannot be a real man if you are doing negative stuff and demonstrate negative character traits. If you want to be a real man, you must demonstrate that you have character, style, and a sense of responsibility. You must also show you have a strong work ethic, follow through on your commitments, and are a productive member of society.

MAKING SACRIFICES

Real men work! They go to school, start businesses, earn degrees, and give back to society. They are self-sufficient. In order to be self-sufficient, you will need to make some significant sacrifices. Real men chose to make sacrifices; boys do not. You can't run the streets with your friends, hanging out getting high, drinking, and chasing women all the time, and still plan on getting ahead. You can't focus on that stuff and at the same time focus on keeping a job, moving up in corporate America, or building your own business. It doesn't work that way.

Is it more fun to hang out with friends, or go to a math tutor to learn calculus? The answer is easy; it's more fun to hang out with friends. But the difference is more than likely, the guy who spent time with his tutor, will earn significantly more money than the one who hung out with his friends. More than likely, the young man who chose to hang out with his friends is still doing so in their homes and local sports bars as a grown man. The other one is doing so with his friends in the Caribbean, Europe, Vegas, and much other nicer places. It all depends on what you want and how badly you're willing to work to get it.

I'm not saying you can't spend time with your friends and still get ahead. I am saying that you may need to make some tough choices and sacrifices while you are young that help you get to where you want to go when you are older. It is about balance. You can have it all; you just may not be able to have it all at the same time.

You won't be able to spend one hundred percent of your time dating and then turn around and spend one hundred percent of your time working, studying, playing sports or partying. Again, life doesn't work that way, and there simply isn't enough time.

VULNERABILITY

Being a man is also about having the ability to show weaknesses.

Only a fool will remain lost for an extended period of time without asking for help or directions! As men, we need to understand our limitations and learn how to ask for assistance, especially when it comes to our health. Too many of us often feel something is wrong, yet are too afraid to find out what it is or share it with someone.

Personally, I'd rather go to the doctor and find out what is wrong than wait too late and find out I'm going to die. Most of the time, it isn't that drastic, but we can still put off going to the doctor long enough for illnesses to cause our lifestyle to change. This is part of being responsible, not only to ourselves, but to our families.

Being a man is about making tough choices and decisions. It isn't about showboating for your friends and neighbors by going out and buying material items, you know darn well you can't afford. It is about living within your means, not someone else's. If you try that, you will fail. It's only a matter of how soon and how low you will go, but you're going! Please don't make this choice.

You may feel embarrassed because you aren't driving the latest cool car or living in the best community. Well, if so, then think about how embarrassed you'll feel after getting your cool car repossessed or evicted from your home or apartment in that nice community. The last two are entirely different levels of embarrassment.

My point is; there are real men out there who do struggle. The fact you are out there trying your best, seeking to better yourself and your family; is what makes you a man. Some men work all their lives and yet never quite reach the ability to relax financially. That doesn't mean they aren't men, or they aren't successful. Each one of us has different starting points in life and, for this reason, may cause us to define success differently. You will need to define what it is for you. The key will be to make sure it is your definition and not someone else's. Doing so is critical to your happiness and success.

DRUNK OR HIGH

I know you see some guys now, or you may see some in a few years, who are always "high or drunk." Yet, they somehow manage to stay in school, hold down good jobs, or successfully run their own businesses. Some of them who demonstrate negative behaviors may drive nice cars and own nice homes. They are the exception to the rule and often what you see is an illusion, because, behind the scenes, their lives are a mess. What you don't realize, and perhaps they don't either, is most of them are only one or two incidents away from losing everything. One drunk driving arrest, one drug possession arrest, one pissed off woman or friend, and poof, their whole world is gonna change, and not for the better.

SHORT TERM vs. LONG TERM THINKING

I'm sure you've seen names of some sports figures, CEOs or Congressmen, who've lost their jobs over greed, laziness, or plain stupidity. In most cases, their money is gone and so is their short-lived glory. Some people are "just glad to get there." They are happy to make a team, become the CEO, or become a politician. That is where their goals stopped.

For others, they want to remain in their attained position. For them, getting the job or getting onto the team was not their end goal. They didn't do all of that hard work to be removed a few months or few years later. They want to bear all of the fruits of their labor and ride their financial increase and competitive journey for as long as they can. Do you see the difference in vision?

The bottom line is these men: made sacrifices, smart choices, developed good habits, are consistent, have long-term goals, and they work hard. They aren't just "in it for the minute" and they don't throw their careers away by being self-destructive.

Lesson 3.

What is Success?
Defining it and having it

"The two most important days in your life are the day you are born and the day you find out why."

~ *Mark Twain*

"The road to success is dotted with many tempting parking spaces."

~ *Unknown*

DAD'S DEFINITION OF SUCCESS

For me, success is based on finding something you enjoy doing and being able to get paid to do it. It's based on one's relationship with God, family, and friends. It's based on one's character, integrity, and ability to provide for his family without daily financial stress. It is based on staying in tune with life's rhythm. Additionally, it is based on some unknown, awful day, having the ability to make the right choice and stick with it, even when I know it goes against what everyone else is doing. With the above foundation, you will have success. You will be able to look at yourself in the mirror without feeling ashamed.

I do believe success happens when preparation meets opportunity. This is another saying I like. Success also happens because you consistently surround yourself with supportive, encouraging friends/family, co-workers, and you are willing to do the work that many are not. It happens because you put effort into consistently learning and adapting to your ever changing environment. Further, no matter how many failures you have, you keep trying. Success is often a choice that requires numerous sacrifices of something; time, fun, sleep, or a combination of them.

As an example, I know of a professional musician who gets up every morning at 6 a.m. to practice for two hours, no matter how late he went to bed. He practices for two more hours at a different point in his day. He does this every day, and people love his music! But they have no idea what it means to practice hard for four hours every single day. He does this with such discretion that most don't even know about it. He goes out to dinners, attends events and when everyone else is going to bed; that's when he's practicing. He practices over one thousand hours a year, every year and earns a good living doing something he enjoys. Not everyone can say that.

SUCCESS DOES NOT EQUATE TO CHARACTER

Some may read the chapter, Becoming A Real Man, and dismiss it. They may even throw out names of men they know who they feel are successful. The key words here are "men who they feel are successful." The important question is; what is your definition of being a successful man? Is it driving nice cars? Is it living in big homes? Being a multi-millionaire or billionaire? Having a large number of material things?

If these things are what you define success by, then you've missed the boat because there are other more important things. Can you be trusted? How does your family see you? How do your friends see you? How does God see you? How do you see yourself when you look in the mirror? What's your character like?

Character has nothing to do with money or material possessions. Working and saving will get you that. Character has to do with holding yourself accountable for your actions or lack of actions. It has to do with owning up to your mistakes, learning from them, and putting in place changes in your lifestyle that will keep you from making those same mistakes for the same reasons. It is also about your spiritual growth and the journey you choose to take in this life.

Many millionaires are miserable. Many middle or lower class people are very happy. Money will not make you happy, although we know a lack of enough money can lead to bitterness, fear, and resentment. It is about choice. Your choice. What do you want for yourself? How are you going to define success for yourself? The main thing is for you to find your comfort level.

If you want to be a millionaire, you probably are going to have to work substantially more than the standard forty-hour week to get there. You will have to save and invest. That is how many millionaires got to be millionaires. And, by the way, it's one thing to become a millionaire; it's an entirely different thing to stay one. This too will require sacrifices.

Subsequently, if you want to work forty hours a week or less so you can spend more time with your family or avoid corporate pressure, more than likely, your financial picture may look different. You may not be able to afford all of the latest and greatest, i.e., tennis shoes, concerts, or cars. Most forty hour a week jobs simply don't put you on the path to becoming a millionaire without you doing significant saving and investing. You may still be able to buy some expensive items and live a comfortable lifestyle, but you'll need to make good plans, save money diligently, and invest wisely.

This isn't to say there aren't any great paying, forty-hour work week jobs that provide a great salary because there are. In order to obtain one, you'll need to start by choosing a college major that leads to solid employment in one of them. Again, planning is key. Actuary positions, petroleum engineers, some attorney positions, dentists, and eye doctors, are a few careers offering great salaries with reasonable work hours. You'll have to do the research to find what works for you.

BALANCE

Success requires balance. For years, Phil Mickelson, a world-renowned golfer, was known as "the best golfer to never win a major." That is until 2004. You can read up on all of the glowing stories about him after that year, but I want to focus on him prior to that. Although some would argue he wasn't successful before then, I'd argue he was. Why; because Phil has a strong sense of family. He is a professional golfer, but he also is a loving and more importantly "present" father for his children and husband to his wife. By "present" I mean he is involved and active, not a father who spends time with his children when it is only convenient for him, or for a photo op.

He is one of the people I respect simply because he has balance with his work and family. There are several other excellent examples of people who have this balance, but I picked him because he stands out for me. He has been criticized for not practicing golf more so he would be better and win majors. Regardless, Phil chose to spend time with his family and decided that was just as important as being a pro-golfer. Because of his choices, I believe it took him longer to become the great golfer he is now and gain notoriety.

Look at it from this perspective; golf is a sport, family is your responsibility, your life duty, and a gift from God. Nothing will be more important on your death bed than being with your family and close friends. Your job will not come visit you when you are ill or dying. Your job will not help nurse you back to health. Your job will not take care of your mental fragility when bad times occur. Your job certainly won't replace all of the time you lost playing with your children, vacationing with family, attending family events, or just spending daily time with them. What your job will do is sit and wait for the next person to step in and take your place when you are gone. It won't miss you, and it doesn't need you, but your family does, and they will miss you when you're gone.

FEARING, DREAMING, AND TRYING

Another message I want to drive home is, don't fear success so much that you don't try. I know a number of people whose fear of success exceeds their fear of failure. For example, rather than risking the possibility of, not making a sports team, not getting the promotion, or not getting accepted into a college, they decided not to even try.

They feared if they went out for the team, they might not make it. They feared if they did make a team, they might screw up and never play. They feared if they got a promotion, they might not do well. They feared that if they got into a college, they might flunk out.

In fact, they feared those things so much, they never bothered to consider seriously what could happen if they succeeded. What if they made the team, took the promotion, or went to college and did well?

Often, fear shows up in the forms of; lack of confidence, lack of faith, or low self-esteem. It can also show up because you lack experience. For example, because you've never made the basketball team before, you fear you won't make it this time, or if you do, you'll fail miserably and get cut. But once you get some experience under you; e.g., learning how to shoot, dribble, box out, you gain more confidence in your abilities. How can you ever gain more confidence if you never practice or try out in the first place?

Speaker/Author, Elizabeth Gilbert, who wrote *Eat, Pray, Love*, stated, "Your fear is the most boring thing about you." I love this! What she talks about is how our fear is the least important thing about any of us because we all have it. She goes on to elaborate on how fear isn't what makes us who we are unless we choose to let it. It is us as individuals, choosing to allow fear to control us when in reality; each of us is so much more than that.

What if Beethoven never tried to play the piano because of fear? What if Luther Vandross, Whitney Houston, Mariah Carey or Frank Sinatra never attempted to sing? What if Larry Bird, Magic Johnson, LeBron James or Peyton Manning never tried to play sports? What if Peyton Manning never attempted to come back after his neck surgeries? I'm sure you get the picture. Each of us is born with talent and a purpose to do something. The struggle is figuring out what our talent is and then having the willingness, courage, determination, and consistency to develop it into something that we can make a living doing.

One of my favorite athletes, Russell Wilson, quarterback for the NFL's Seattle Seahawks, has a commercial. In it, he says, "dreams don't happen, dreams are made." I love this too! It is so on point and it means that dreams are a function of work! Every night, you can lie down in bed and dream about whatever you want. You can even daydream, but the reality is unless you do something, nothing is going to happen. If you start dreaming about something at seventeen and do nothing, by the time you're seventy, you may very well be dreaming those same dreams. What a shame and waste of time, especially when you had every opportunity to get out there and make your dream a reality.

You can start making your dreams happen by posting a picture of something you want to achieve on your bathroom mirror and look at it every morning. You can post a phrase, look at it, and repeat it daily. Do something about your dream today! Any little thing! Make a step! The saying, "a journey of 1,000 miles started with one step" is true. Start stepping!

Sometimes it helps to think of those less fortunate. Think of a poor immigrant living in a third world country with; little food, no heat, no air conditioning, filthy living conditions, and a brutal government. Yet, they have a dream of coming to America. When they get here, they start working as a janitor or house cleaner, cleaning filthy bathrooms so they can move up. They are driven; even excited because they are here and feel they are on their way up! They attend night school to learn English or get more skills. They dream about getting their family over here and eventually, they do. They buy a business or get a good paying job and continue to increase their quality of life. They now look back on what they have achieved and smile. You can too!

You can choose the lens through which you want to see the world. You can look at the filth and nastiness of cleaning the toilets and wallow in that, or you can look at the beauty of it providing you an opportunity to bring your family over to the United States.

You can look around and see or listen to others talk about negative things going on in the world; racism, inequality, discrimination, sexism, or horrible judicial system cases. You can even choose to let them drag you down. Admittedly, several of those things have affected and hurt me.

They have impacted the amount of money I make and have negatively impacted my quality of life.

Despite all of that, I made up my mind when I was 17 years old that no matter what negative stuff is thrown at me, I'm going to fight and I'm going to win! Failure is not an option! There are some things that happened to me which have set me back, but I've been determined to get back up on my feet. Sometimes I've needed encouragement and faith to do so, but I've done it.

DON'T GIVE UP

Don't choose to adopt a "victim mentality." Doing so will only make you a victim! Choose to "minimize" the negative impact bad things have on your state of mind and keep pushing forward.

A famous jazz singer, Diane Reeves, shared at a concert I attended that her mother says something to the effect of; "I may get illnesses or the blues, but I don't entertain them." In other words, what she's stating is that while she may get sick or depressed, those will only be temporary; she's not keeping them around. Do you see what a difference her thought process makes? It can have a tremendous impact on the quality of your life.

Our school system teaches us we need to be 90% successful all of the time in order to get an "A" grade or 80% successful to get a "B" grade. In real life, that honestly isn't true. In fact, it's a huge lie! In most cases, we are led to believe if we don't get 90% or above, we aren't that good or perhaps we are even failures.

Since many students have been taught this, when they go to a major university or college and don't get A's, they quit. It's sad. Thomas Edison made over 4,000 experiments that were not the light bulb. The guys who started LinkedIn had made their pitch to over 300 Venture Capitalists before they found one who would fund them. Many professional baseball players hitting .330 or 33% of the pitches thrown to them make over $15M a year. A professional salesman who makes a pitch to 100 prospects and only closes 10 sales is considered very successful. The point is that an 80 to 90% success rate requirement in the real world is very unusual and an exception, not the rule.

Nevertheless, there are exceptions. There are things we should expect to work all the time. Medication, airplanes, cars, medical devices; are some obvious things that better have a success rate approaching 100%! But I'm not talking about those things. I'm talking about what happens when you try new things, perform experiments or create art. These are the types of things that won't have and don't need an 80 to 90% success rate in order for you to be considered a success.

There are people who do nothing except buy a lottery ticket and become instant millionaires. It happens. But do you know anyone who has had this happen? Realistically, do you think that is all you need to do? Just wake up every day, go to the store, buy a lottery ticket, and then go back home and wait for your ship to come in? Very, very, very few people win millions in the lottery and many who do go broke within three years.

Buying lottery tickets is gambling on someone else's game. Simply put, I'd rather gamble and bet on you! That is a winning bet, and I'm proud to do it. What I hope you believe is that you'd rather invest your time, energy, and money in you. I hope you'd rather work on creating your future, rather than sitting back and waiting and hoping a very particular set of numbers comes up positive on a lottery ticket. Your chances of success are significantly higher if you work to create your own success and make your dreams a reality. I hope you do just that!

Lesson 4.

The Rhythm of Life

The importance of discovering your own rhythm

"Everything Must Change" ~ title of a song by George Benson

LIFE'S RHYTHM

There is a rhythm to life. The four seasons are rhythmic; the rain, the snow, the sun, the moon, the warmth, the cold. George Benson, a famous jazz guitarist, had a song entitled "Everything Must Change." It speaks eloquently to the rhythm of life.

When announcers speak about particular teams or players who are struggling, they frequently mention the need for them to get into a "rhythm." Your heartbeat has a rhythm. Your walk has a rhythm. Music has a rhythm. Machines, cars and motorcycles, all have rhythms. Most things that have engines or motors have rhythms.

My point is everyone has a rhythm to their own life and the key to success is figuring out what that rhythm is and then staying on its beat. When you are out of rhythm with life, you will probably not be happy or successful. Sometimes you may find yourself with a large number of distractions going on in your life. Trying to stay focused when this happens can be difficult or impossible. When you are arguing with your girlfriend, having disagreements with your parents/siblings, or feeling used by friends, it's hard to stay focused on your own rhythm.

Sometimes you will have to stop and fix relationships, change your conduct at work, or take time out to study or practice. As soon as possible though, you must get back to focusing on getting in tune with your life's rhythm. Figuring out your rhythm is important. Keeping your rhythm is even more important.

In basketball, announcers talk about a player "shooting himself out of a slump." Life is no different. You may have pitfalls, trials, and depression. None the less, you will need to keep stepping and keep moving forward. That is the only way to "shoot yourself out of those slumps." The alternative is failure.

THE DIFFERENCE BETWEEN FAILING VS. FAILURE

Don't confuse "failing" with "failure." Failure can be a finality, where failing can be a specific point along a path to success. When you first try to make a basket, you will probably fail, but in the end, you'll learn how to shoot and make them frequently. This is one example of the difference between failing and failure.

When you are in a deep slump, you probably will not be able to see how things can get better. You may ask yourself, "so why should I try?" I can answer that. You should try because God instilled a heart within you and within that heart He instilled courage, drive, and perseverance.

As a child, you went from looking around, to rolling over, to crawling, standing, and eventually walking. The first time you walked wasn't the first time you tried. You tried several times and trust me, you failed miserably. Do you know it takes a child about a thousand hours of trying before they actually walk successfully?[1] Without knowing it, even as little babies, we kept trying over and over again to accomplish our goal of walking. Still, most people only try something about three times before they give up.

How critical is walking in life? Very critical! While some people have learned to get around very well without that essential ability, having it sure makes things a heck of a lot easier. Just think if you'd given up trying to walk after three attempts! You were a determined winner from the beginning, but the world tries to talk you out of that determination. Keep it!

DON'T GET STUCK

Overcoming failure is instilled within us, without us even knowing it. Build on that. Each of us experienced critical failures and setbacks early in our lives, for something that was vital to our lives. The majority of us overcame those failures.

Whenever you experience difficulties and challenges, stop whatever you are doing and focus on what that difficulty or challenge is. These are crucial moments. Ask yourself; is there something you could have done to avoid this? What can you change? What else can you do? What might you do differently next time? Think about something you overcame in your past, how you made it through, and how you can apply those same actions to your current situation. Sometimes you absolutely will not see the light at the end of the tunnel. But, just because you can't see it, doesn't mean it isn't there.

KNOWING SOMETHING EXISTS THAT YOU CAN'T SEE

Pastor Chris Hill, from *The Potter's House of Denver*, had a beautiful analogy I'd like to share. During one of his sermons, he talked about being in a dark room that had a light switch on the other side he couldn't see. He talked about how he started moving toward that light switch. He stepped forward slowly, hands extended outward, gently trying to feel objects that might be in his way. Slowly, he kept moving forward step by step until eventually, he found the switch. He said that is called faith. It is knowing that a light switch is there, not being able to see it, but still seeking and moving toward it. That is what each of us needs to do when bad things happen. We each have an obligation to ourselves to keep pushing forward in order to discover, connect, or even re-connect with our rhythm of life.

Lesson 5.

Relationships with Women
The do's and don'ts

"The grass always looks greener on the other side, however, more often than not, once you get over there you will find you are standing on Astroturf."

~ Unknown

"There are two types of women in the world; those who want healthy, mutually beneficial relationships and those who don't. Forget what they tell you, let their actions show you."

~ David Dixon

LEARN TO RECOGNIZE GOOD WOMEN

The best advice I can give you is: quickly figure out what a good young lady is and what a good young lady is not. Learn to recognize the differences and don't fool with the other types. Some females are good, some are bad, and some are just plain scandalous, deceitful, conniving, and manipulative. When you recognize those character traits; run, don't just walk away!

On the other side of the coin, more often than not, behind every good man, is a wonderful, solid, loving and caring woman. She is a champion, a helper, a partner, and super power in his life. This is the type of woman you should want and strive to find.

All the same, before you get there, you need to understand this; men have two heads. Make sure you think with the one on top of your shoulders because if the other drives you, as it can, you may find yourself in a world of trouble! Believe me when I say all that glitters is not gold. Every fine, attractive young lady you see who looks good on the outside doesn't necessarily look as fine and attractive on the inside!

THE BEST TYPE OF WOMAN FOR YOU

I want to strongly encourage you to think long and hard about the type of woman you want and then compare that with the type of woman you need. Sometimes there are drastic differences. I'm speaking from personal experience and it is something I struggled with for years. The type of woman I am attracted to, quite frankly, isn't good for me, and it took me years to figure that out. No, I don't feel like I have "settled" by choosing the type of woman that is good for me. I finally figured out I could have it all; beauty, brains, and personality. I also realized in order to do so, I had to become more mature and take more time before deciding to jump into a relationship.

There are certain questions you need to ask yourself about the young lady's you meet. How deep is she? Is she interested in me as much as I am in her? How does she manage anger? How responsible is she? Does she lie? Does she treat me the same way in public as she does in private? What are her friends like? (Often this can give you substantial insight into her character.)

THE IMPORTANCE OF DATING

Although it took some time and dating around to get this point, I've become smarter about dating as I've gotten older. Initially, I didn't recognize I had an issue with dating the wrong types of women. I'm probably not alone. I doubt most men go out and immediately start dating the right kinds of women who are the best for them. That is why it's called "dating." Most guys I know had to learn how to date and make better choices in selecting women they get along well with.

To be clear, when I say, "learn," I'm not just talking about you learning how to make better choices in selecting women you want to date. I am talking about you learning how to be a better man and better at dating period. You'll have to learn what discussions or arguments are worth the effort and energy. Most arguments are simply not that important and you will need to learn when to let them go. You will have to learn to compromise on some things and be more flexible on others, based on what you find you need in a relationship.

Like most things in life, this is a journey. You will have to continuously learn from your mistakes and poor choices until you figure it out. Hopefully, you will also leverage the knowledge you've learned from watching me make some of my mistakes. Nevertheless, be patient with yourself. No one can expect to be a good painter, driver, artist or mathematician if they've only tried each of them three or four times.

Knowing the difference between the types of women you want or are attracted to, versus the types of women you need and who are good for you, takes some emotional maturity. You can have both; just know you have to keep your head on top of your shoulders in charge. If you do that, I promise you, your quality of life will be substantially better.

You will have to work at having a quality relationship. You will also have to define what a quality relationship is for you.

It is important that you choose a young lady who has balance. This would be the type of young lady who cares just as much about her hair as her heart. This would be the kind of young lady who cares as much about her nails, makeup, clothes, and shoes, as her soul and inner beauty. Each of us has something known as our "essence." Your essence is who you are as a man and her essence is who she is as a young lady. You want a young lady who has an essence that resembles yours and who brings out the best in you. These are the best pieces of advice I can share with you, along with some rules below:

RULE ONE: DATE YOUNG WOMEN NOT WHORES

I know this sounds harsh, but it's true; date young women, not whores. (A little side note for you; men can be whores too! Don't you be one!) A whore is generally referred to as a person who sleeps around with little discretion. Any man can have a whore, that's why they call them whores. Keep in mind there are several other variations of whores, not just the sexual ones. There are those who are only concerned about: getting money, manipulating people, playing games, doing drugs, and the list goes on. These types of women are nothing special, nor do they deserve you. They come a dime a dozen and frankly, can be very distracting. Develop the right radar to recognize them. Say hello and keep it moving.

Many young ladies will be willing to share their bodies with you. What you need to understand is that more often than not, they are sharing their bodies with other men while also sharing other things with you; like sexually transmitted diseases. Don't think some young lady is doing you a favor because she "puts out." Chances are if she is putting out for you, she's putting out for others too.

I'm truly sorry to bust your bubble, but to the above types of women, son, you are just not that special. This is the problem with many young and even older men; we think we are significantly more special than we are. We believe our smooth talking ways are so much better than the next guy's. When in actuality, the young ladies we are hooking up with are just as indiscriminate about who they choose to sleep with as many of us. These young ladies are looking for a man to hook up with and you fit the bill. Once she gets what she wants, she'll be gone; although that doesn't mean she may not leave you with something you don't want or can't get rid of. Do not get it twisted!

RULE TWO: USE CHIVALRY

There is a word I'd like you to familiarize yourself thoroughly with; chivalrous. Use it! The definition of chivalrous, as defined by Merriam-Webster Dictionary is: "behaving in an honorable or polite way especially toward women." You need to understand the women I just mentioned would never appreciate you or your acts of chivalry. Some might "use" you, but they'd never "appreciate" you. Keep that in mind.

You want someone special because you are someone special. Open doors, assist with putting on her coat. Let her go into a building or come out of an elevator first. Walk on the curb side of the street. Let her order first at restaurants and yes, it is perfectly okay and expected that you pay for some meals, movie tickets, etc. The key word here being "some", not all.

Relationships are an investment both people need to contribute too. If you find a woman whose expectation is that you pay for everything all the time, this woman is not for you. I am quite sure this will cause some disagreement among some women, especially some raised in other cultures. That is fine, but you have to know your limitations and vocalize them. The last time I checked, you are not a bank, open for withdrawal at any woman's convenience. Don't fall for that.

RULE THREE: UNDERSTAND YOUR MONEY

This rule transitions nicely from the previous one. Pay careful attention to a woman who allows you to spend your money freely without ever offering to spend hers. Sure, a man should know his own wallet. This is why you budget. She doesn't know your wallet, for this reason, if she is kind and caring, she will at least "check in" with you. She will ask if she can order something expensive on the menu. At a minimum, she will double-check with you to make sure you are comfortable with the prices. This is called reality, respect, and compassion. It should come like a breath of fresh air. Relish it.

For her to be completely okay with the assumption that if you are spending money without any sensitivity to the amount you are spending, in my opinion, shows a lack of respect for you. Women know men spend money to impress them and they are also well aware men overspend to do so. For this reason, having some empathy, concern, or care, should be a part of her psyche. If it isn't, don't let the doorknob hit you on the way out.

You see, son, by always spending your money, it becomes an expectation, not appreciation. It becomes a "rule" or a "standard" in how your relationship with her operates. Down the road, should you ever wind up in financial trouble, this type of woman will be gone. You were her "cash flow", not her man. You can't expect her to stay around, nor can you expect her to help you. Those would be unreasonable expectations because she never had to do either in the past. You all were never a team. You were her provider and she took.

I don't want you to allow yourself to be used. You know your finances. Don't act like you can afford something you can't and don't spend money you don't have. I know this can be tough. We'd all like to walk into a restaurant or car dealership and order whatever we want, but very few people can afford to do that. Even the wealthiest people I know check the prices. Why; because most of them didn't earn their wealth by being foolish with their money. Set boundaries for yourself and you'll be fine.

I'm sure you are familiar with the word "perpetrating." The problem with perpetrating is you are misleading a woman into thinking you are something you are not. Sooner or later, she will find out and when she does, she'll be gone. Then you may be really hurt and probably angry, but you'd have no one to be angry with but yourself.

You weren't honest with her and now that she's gone, it's costing you. Worse still, all of the money you spent on her over the past months or years, you might as well have flushed down the toilet because it's gone too. There was no return on that investment or at the least, not the type you were expecting.

RULE FOUR: KEEP IT REAL

"The same thing it took to get your woman hooked, it's going to take the same thing to keep her." Those are lyrics from a popular seventy's song by the Impressions, and some of that is absolutely true! Earlier I talked about consistency and being yourself. Consider the frustration you've experienced when you've gone to a store because they've advertised an item, but when you get there, they don't have it and try to offer you something else? Well, that's called "bait and switch." No woman wants that and you don't either. You can't start out one way, doing things to attract her to you, then switch and start doing things differently later and expect her to stay. Consistency is the key.

Be yourself and be upfront and honest with the young ladies you date. If they aren't doing the same, don't worry, eventually they will show you who they truly are. They can't help themselves and neither can you. Eventually, the real you will come out. Trying to be something you are not to get a woman is a waste of time; hers and yours. Eventually, you are going to consciously or unconsciously want to revert back to being exactly who you are and then she may leave. For this reason, you might as well be yourself from the start so she knows who she's dealing with. Have the same expectation for her as well.

This doesn't mean you don't put forth your best effort and go out of your way to get her attention. That's just good sense. Still, when you try to act as if you like things you don't, or eat things you don't like, then you are giving the impression you are someone who you are not. Inevitably, problems will set in because you'll get tired of acting and she'll feel duped. The result is you will have pain, anger, and drama to deal with and it won't be fun.

This same rule should apply to women you date. If you feel they are superficial, then avoid committing to a relationship. Those women are not for you. You can avoid some of the above issues if, from the beginning of the relationship, you speak up. If she is mad because you can't afford to take her to a nice restaurant now, then the reality is she will not be around for you to take her to one later. Even if she does hang around for a while, if this is her expectation and you can't do it consistently, she will eventually leave you for another man who can. That's a fact.

At the most fundamental level, this is about food. We can eat cheaply. It would be nice to eat well and even eat expensively once in a while. But if expensive and money is all she is about, then she needs to find someone else and you need to move on.

If you are only interested in dating and not having a serious relationship with her, be upfront. Go have a good time together, but with no pretense. Don't use, abuse or mistreat women. Women don't deserve that. No one wants to be hurt, so don't play games. Think about how you'd feel if she was playing games with you.

If you realize she is playing games, leave. It isn't even worth your time trying to get back at her. That time could be spent on searching for someone better. There is no benefit in wasting time on someone you know you don't want or for that matter, you know doesn't want you. Just look forward. Let those types go. Life will deal with them in its own time.

RULE FIVE: BEING ALONG VS. BEING IN A RELATIONSHIP

Great relationships require energy, consistency, nurturing, emotional availability, and acceptance. It is doubtful you will ever like everything about your mate. That's just the way it is. There are some things you can tolerate in mates and some things you can't or won't. You'll have to figure out what those are for yourself.

One thing I know is this; having a consistent temperament is one of the essential attributes of a successful relationship. Doing some things you don't want but that she enjoys helps. Making time to give her your undivided attention helps. Doing each of these will strengthen a relationship.

As you get older, you'll have many things going on that can interfere with a relationship. You'll have to decide when the right time is for you to be in a relationship, and it may not be all the time. If you are trying to finish school and are loading up on classes or working eighty-plus hours a week at work, this might not be the best time to enter into a relationship.

You have to be able to commit time and energy if you want a meaningful relationship. Seeing someone a few times a week or a month will generally cause a relationship to end. It may work for a while when you're both busy, but sooner or later, one of you is going to have free time. When that happens, one of you is going to want to spend more time together. If both of you can't commit to doing this or don't want to, the relationship is doomed.

There generally always seems to be a significant amount of pressure on men to have a woman; often a very attractive woman they can show off. Remember what I mentioned before. Attraction is not just what is on the outside, but what is on the inside as well. Don't let others define who you should be with and why.

If you are about something, then it is expected that you have a woman on your arms. If you don't, then the assumption is something must be wrong with you. Don't let this type of pressure force you into making bad decisions and choices. You will not always have a girlfriend or someone you are dating. It is an unreasonable and unrealistic expectation. If you bring someone to an event just to have her on your arm, you may miss getting that new girlfriend who is there alone, looking for someone like you. Worse than not having a woman and feeling lonely, is having one just for the sake of it, and still feeling lonely. Your dad's been there and done that as well.

Make sure you don't enter into a relationship of convenience and mistakenly assume it is something different. At times, relationships can be just that; convenient. You have the same classes, live on the same block, or you both are in between relationships. This doesn't necessarily mean the person cares about you.

Learn to feel comfortable being alone. There is nothing wrong with spending time with yourself. Learn to love yourself and enjoy your "me time." I've gone to nice restaurants for dinner by myself plenty of times and enjoyed my own company. I've also gone to the movies by myself. Sure, you will get bored sometimes and have lonely feelings but you will learn to manage them. That is a much better alternative than being with a woman you aren't interested in but staying with only because you don't want to be lonely.

Being alone can have numerous benefits if you use that time wisely. You can get to know yourself better, build upon your spirituality, read, or just spend time cultivating your life and career. Perhaps you can focus on building a business. You can spend time creating an image in your mind of the type of woman you want to meet and how you are going to position yourself to do that.

Many years ago, a friend of mine in California got lonely and met a woman he didn't care about. (He gave me permission to write about this in general terms.) They had unprotected sex and she became pregnant with his child. He is now attached to a woman who, he not only doesn't know, but he doesn't like. He is now married to someone else. But, unfortunately, this other woman will be in his and all of his family's lives, as well as in his pocket receiving child support for many years to come. Understand that short-term joy and short-term bad decisions can have long-term significant consequences.

Being alone and learning how to manage your time or loneliness is much better than creating a child with some woman you don't care about and dealing with the consequences and challenges that follow. One way to avoid this is always choosing to think with the head on your shoulders!

On the positive side, meeting a great woman is wonderful. If the relationship goes well and you start to think about marriage, that's great too. I'd like to encourage you to think about dating for at least a year before you pop the question. People can put on facades for quite some time, but at about the three to six-month mark, they can't help but to start showing themselves for whom they are. They get tired of the charade. Look for those changes and pay close attention to what she does and less attention to what she says. Actions speak louder than words.

You may be in a relationship that is going perfectly for three to six months or longer, and you'll think about what I've said and written and want to ignore it and marry your girl anyway. Well, you can certainly do that, but let me ask you this; if things are going so great at this point, then why wouldn't they continue going great for another six months?

Unless she is being deployed overseas for some long-term assignment, what's the rush? Getting married or having someone move in are very significant decisions and need to be thoroughly thought out. Rushing into relationships and marriages can have awful consequences that could have been avoided had you waited.

If you chose to do this, potentially, there may be bigger issues that may take a lot longer than three to six months to resolve. So don't rush into marriage or cohabitation. It's not worth the risk to you, your personal belongings, or your mental and emotional well-being. If a girlfriend starts to pressure you, perhaps that may be a signal it is time for you to walk away.

Let me give you an example of "things going wrong." You decide to rush into a relationship and either get married or move your girlfriend in. After doing so, you find out she's completely irresponsible about taking care of home belongings and within six months you realize the money you were hoping to save is being spent on replacing or fixing items. You also discover she has a nasty attitude and has significant issues with trust and jealousy. Now you've decided you want her to move out but are concerned about how to get her to do so without her damaging your property.

Let me share with you an example of "things going great." You meet the woman of your dreams. You connect, you feel at peace. The two of you share similar likes and dislikes. You treat each other with respect. She appreciates you and tells you often. Her actions and words state you are a priority in her life. She takes care of you mentally, emotionally, and physically. It's all good, and the relationship is only at the nine-month mark. Now what?!

Love is powerful and beautiful when it is right. What can help make it right is for you to have taken the time to know yourself. You need to know what is important to you, what you value, and what you believe. You also need to have a relationship with God. If you do these things, they will help you know when it's the right time to move forward towards marriage.

I proposed to my soul mate sooner than my "self-created" benchmark of one year. I questioned myself and I communicated openly with her. I was nervous and even a bit scared. But I can tell you, son, I spent time doing the work on myself, and walking in faith, which led me to make one of the best decisions of my life. I didn't know how to do this properly when I was in my twenty's or thirty's. That is why I had my self-created one-year rule. Generally speaking, as you get older, you get wiser. So some of the rules I created earlier can be deviated from to a degree as you get older.

Relationships can be complicated and love even more so, but they don't have to be. Ultimately, what I want for you is to find the love of your life who honors and respects you as a man and as her partner. You may dig through some mud before you find your diamond, but trust me, you will find her.

RULE SIX: WHEN TO WALK AWAY

Know when to walk away. There is a particular saying I like. "A 'SHIP' is designed to take you places; if your companionSHIP, friendSHIP, or relationSHIP, isn't taking you anywhere, then it is time to abandon SHIP." I urge you to keep this in mind as you move forward in life. Notice this saying isn't specifically applicable to relationships with women; it applies to all relationships period!

Get a soul mate or helpmate, not a leg weight. Your girlfriend should be someone who you can lean on at times. She should be someone who you trust and confide in. She should be your best friend. You should be able to look back after a year of dating her and notice self-improvement based on her being in your life. You should have enough sense to want to grow and develop and so should she. If you've seen no growth in yourself or her, then I'd suggest you re-examine your relationship. You should be trying to make each other better people and be willing to do the work to get you both there.

Strive for healthy, mutually beneficial relationships. Some relationships are mutually beneficial, but they are not healthy; like a drug addict and drug dealer's relationship. It's mutually beneficial but not healthy. Apply it to all of your relationships, not just your girlfriends. If you do this, you'll be better off and have a more enriching life.

Sometimes walking away from a bad relationship can be hard. You'd think it would be easy, but it's anything but. This can happen for a number of reasons, the biggest being that usually rationalization sets in. The power of one's ability to rationalize something bad as being something good is incredible! I've done it. I look back at how I came up with some of my decision and have wondered what it was I could have possibly been thinking.

There are other factors as well that make leaving difficult. Perhaps you became comfortable or you like her family. Perhaps you are close friends with her brother or you all run with the same group of friends. Perhaps she's beautiful to look at, has a great sense of humor, and lavishes you with lovely gifts you couldn't afford to buy yourself. Maybe she makes more money than you, drives a nicer car or even lives in a better apartment or home. Therefore, you have access to all of that. Perhaps the sex is great. These are all things that can contribute to your decision to stay in a bad relationship. Focusing on material or sexual things in a relationship, instead of the value of the relationship, in terms of your emotional well-being, can be costly to your health. Doing so can also be just as costly to your ego, self-confidence and a host of other things you may not be considering.

Sometimes relationships just don't work. It doesn't necessarily mean either of you is a bad person, it's just that you don't make a good couple or team. In this situation, there is no need to try to come up with bad things about her or start looking for faults so you have an excuse to leave. You don't have to beat her down mentally and make her feel bad about herself because you are unhappy. It isn't right and it isn't necessary. On the other hand, she might be the "Wicked Witch of the West." Either way, you don't have to belittle her or make her feel bad in order to leave.

In either example, it isn't about her. It is about you. You are unhappy or unsatisfied and want to leave. This is why I ask you to put the work in on yourself first so you know what your limitations are, what your likes and dislikes are, and what you will or will not tolerate. Because now, you have some hard decisions to make and they only get tougher if you don't know yourself.

Choosing to stay in a bad relationship only causes resentment. You may resent her because you feel like she wants you to stay. If you stay, she may resent you because you never told her you wanted to leave. These scenarios go on and on, but the truth is, when someone decides to leave a relationship, the other person gets hurt. Often there is no avoiding it. However, how you choose to exit can make all of the difference in the world.

RULE SEVEN: BECOMING A MAN BEFORE YOUR TIME

Understand that as a man, you are responsible for any child you bring into this world. I believe the time to talk about responsibility and emotional maturity with any young man is now. This is based on what I know, what I have seen, and what I have experienced. I know fourteen-year-old girls (and younger) who have gotten pregnant. Some of those fathers happen to have been thirteen or fourteen year old boys! I'm telling you because I don't want to be that parent who "never thought it could happen to his child." I want you to know right now that it can happen and does happen when you are doing things you don't need to be doing. Don't rush to grow into manhood by making a baby. It's coming. Take your time. Think. Do not put yourself into that position. Let me be frank with you; no matter how hot you think she looks or how easy the process can be, please use your brain.

Understand that manhood requires doing things a man does, not just being a sperm donor. You can't make babies and not change diapers or pay some type of financial support. You can't drive a car and not be able to afford to make the repairs or pay for insurance. You can't own a home or rent an apartment and not pay bills, at least not for long.

When you start acting like a man, you will be expected to absorb the responsibilities of a man. Now is the time for you to start thinking about the choices you and your friends make. Get rid of those who aren't pushing you higher. You need to be your own friend as well and give yourself good advice and counsel. There are consequences for your irresponsible actions and rewards for your responsible ones. I'll get into this more in the next chapter.

RULE EIGHT: LEARN TO SHARE

Don't be selfish. Excellent, healthy relationships require generosity. Give of yourself. You've got to be willing to compromise, listen, and be flexible. If you want to be territorial, you are probably going to be in for some difficult times. If you don't want her using your bathroom, wearing your shirts or socks, driving your car, eating your snacks, then things will probably be challenging. I'm not saying there aren't relationships that work like this because there are. Rather, what I am saying is that you will be looking a lot longer because most women don't like selfish men. Further, most relationships require enough discussions as it is without you adding a selfish element to them. If you do, those discussions and length of them will become significantly more intense and more frequent. This is not what you want.

RULE NINE: PREPARATION

Be prepared. If you are dating someone as a teen, more than likely there will be a time when the discussion about having sex will occur. While I think it would be great if you saved yourself for your wife, realistically, I understand this seriously goes against our culture. But please, please be careful! There is so much that sex does beyond the obvious. You can get diseases that have no cures and you can produce unplanned children. While children are a blessing, they require a significant amount of work, money and time! You are not ready for that!

Having a child is a drastic life changing experience. Don't just take my word for it; ask some of your teenage friends who have children how much their lives have changed. Do not look at sex as pure pleasure, entertainment and fun.

You have significantly more challenges around sexually transmitted diseases than I did when I was your age. There was no AIDS that we, as a society, were aware of when I was fourteen or fifteen. It wasn't even discussed until my junior or senior year in high school. Even then, it was believed that only "gay" people got it. It's interesting to look back on that type of narrow-minded thinking and realize how ignorant and immature we were. We are very fortunate not to have been destroyed by AIDS. But AIDS shouldn't be anyone's only focus. The brutality of Herpes, genital warts, or other sexually transmitted diseases are still powerful and something to be reckoned with.

For you, should you choose to become sexually active, wear protection. Yes, that means a condom. I would also urge you to use discrimination in your choices. Remember, every woman you sleep with has the potential to be the mother of your child. Don't let the heat and lust of the moment override good judgment. This can be a life altering decision. You can sleep with a young lady one time and she can become the mother of your child and have a very significant impact on the quality of the rest of your life. Think about that while you are out there "having fun."

Women can be very sweet, charming and pleasant conversationalists. That is until you piss one of them off, then you'll potentially see a side you never knew existed. Often that side of her might stay around much, much longer after the thrill is gone. Depending on your actions that brought that side of her out, you may never see her good side again. She can be in your arms today and deep in your pockets tomorrow.

Lesson 6.

Candid Conversation
Real talk

"The higher mental development of woman, the less possible it is for her to meet a congenial male who will see in her, not only sex, but also the human being, the friend, the comrade and strong individuality, who cannot and ought not lose a single trait of her character."

~ *Emma Goldman*

"Conservatives say teaching sex education in the public schools will promote promiscuity. With our education system? If we promote promiscuity the same way we promote math or science, they've got nothing to worry about."

~ *Beverly Mickins*

SEX TALK

During one's teen years is the time many discover sex or become very aware of it. We hear about it as children and may have snuck a kiss from someone, but we act on it as teens. Many of our parents talked to us about using protection, avoiding pregnancy and catching sexually transmitted diseases. This is such an awkward conversation for many of us to have with our children. Because of this, too many of us don't get into conversations about the emotional ties that go along with making the decisions to engage in sexual activity. This is unfortunate because it is our emotions that caused us to make those decisions in the first place.

For the majority of people, choosing to have sex carries with it a wealth of emotions. It is very hard to get involved with someone and stay emotionally disconnected. If we were to find a person who was like that, we probably wouldn't want to be with them. In most cases, when we physically connect with someone, we want some type of emotional connection. The majority of relationships have some kind of emotional connection, whether we want to believe it or not.

I know some will argue they've had only physical relationships, but I'd argue that honestly doesn't exist. The ability to have sex starts with an emotion. In most cases, that emotion is an attraction to the person. Even unhealthy emotions like anger or wanting to overpower a person are still emotions that can invoke a physical reaction.

THE IMPORTANCE OF EMOTIONAL MATURITY

When I spoke earlier about becoming a man too soon, this is one of the things I was referring too. You have to be ready both physically and emotionally before you engage in sexual activity. I often speak of emotional maturity; which is critical because with it, comes responsibility and consistency. You have to be responsible enough and mature enough to avoid getting yourself into situations you know you have no business being in. You have to be responsible for protecting yourself all the time. You have to be mature enough to say "no" when you may want to say "yes." You have to have the ability to focus on your end goal. It is very difficult to do that when you're preoccupied with having sexual encounters.

Don't think you can't get someone pregnant because a "friend" told you he's slept with numerous young ladies, and he's never used protection or gotten them pregnant. First of all, he's probably lying. Second, he may not be telling you the whole story. Regardless, that's him, not you. You also need to understand that guys, in general, tend to exaggerate; especially when they start sharing their sexual conquests in a group setting! That seems to be our nature.

Further, don't believe some of your friends when they break up with a girlfriend and tell you everything is fine or they were sick of her anyway. Often they are lying about this too. If either of those things were true, they would have broken up with her, not the other way around. The masochism and bravado you see them display is very often a front for the real pain they are experiencing. You may not find out the truth until you are in a one on one conversation hours, days or even months later.

THE UNKNOWN DEPTHS OF EMOTIONAL PAIN

Very few relationships involving sex are casual or remain casual. Most of the time, someone starts to develop stronger feelings toward the other person more than they did in the beginning and that starts problems. If their partner doesn't reciprocate with the same level of interest, someone is going to get hurt.

When you decide you want to make out with a young lady or take things further, preferably when you get much older, you need to keep in mind the emotional part of those actions. You or she may start out feeling like you've got this part of yourself under control. But once you get into it, you may learn you weren't prepared for the depth of the feelings and emotions you experience.

As a teen or child, you've learned how painful it can be to lose a close friend. But when you add the sexual element to it and then lose that person, it can multiply that pain level exponentially. This is one reason why I believe having sexual experiences too early, should be avoided. It's hard enough to control these emotions we have toward our partners as adults, let alone being a teenager. You only have to look at or listen to the news to know this. Too frequently, we hear stories about relationships gone wrong where couples are being arrested for fighting, shooting, stabbing, or in worse cases, even killing their partner or each other. You also hear about people having mental breakdowns or hurting themselves or their own children when they are unable to deal with the grief of a breakup.

WE'RE MALES – WE CAN HANDLE IT

As males, we often try to act like we are emotionally invincible. If we fall off a bike, get hit by a baseball, beat up by a guy, we attempt to act like we aren't hurting. We jump up, smile, shrug it off and try to hold back the tears until we can get someplace where no one can see us. Much of this is learned behavior from watching other men and hearing sportscasters or friends talk about "how brave and strong" someone was who just got hurt because they "sucked it up."

Perhaps we had our fathers or other important and influential male figures, tell us that our feelings or emotions aren't real. They may have even said things to us like, "Don't be such a baby", "Stop Crying", "Oh come on, it didn't hurt that bad." Or my favorite one, "Do you want me to give you something to cry about?" Comments like this can cause us not to adopt healthy methods for managing our pain. Further, each of us can have very different pain tolerances for various types of pain.

It's not wrong for men or women to be tough. Being tough and sucking it up can be a good thing. It can help you work through stressful situations, increase your pain tolerance, and help you push yourself to better performances in sports. On the other hand, that same behavior can cause us harm when it's overdone. Holding in pain and taking on too much stress can cause high blood pressure, heart attacks, strokes, skin rashes, insomnia, and many other health issues. The need for balance is applicable here.

SUCCESSFUL RELATIONSHIPS REQUIRE SENSITIVITY

When you are dealing with relationships, leave the bravado and machismo out when it comes to managing your feelings. They will not serve you well. The ability to be in tune with what or how you are feeling, as well as how you are making your partner feel, and then being able to express that, will serve you much better.

When your relationship starts turning into a competition of "who can hurt whom first" or paying the other person back for something they did wrong, it's time to leave. This can become a very dangerous game, especially if you start cheating. They can develop their own feelings of attachment or detachment which can lead to confrontations. If either of you starts sleeping around and you are still sleeping with each other, you also increase your risk of exposure to sexually transmitted diseases.

The bottom line is relationships involving sex require emotional maturity and emotional attachment. It is important that you be mindful of that and honor yourself as well as your partner as you move into adulthood.

Lesson 7.

Self-Sabotage
Don't be your worst enemy

"The most powerful words you can ever speak are those you speak to yourself."

~ *Unknown*

"The worst lies are the lies we tell ourselves."

~ *Richard Bach*

YOU ARE WORTHY

If you don't give yourself a chance to be successful, others probably won't either. The worst thing you can do in life is sabotage yourself. Sometimes this happens due to bad habits you create. It is somewhat the equivalent of pouring gas on yourself and setting yourself on fire. Understand that eighty percent of the problems you have in your life will be caused by twenty percent of the things you do wrong. Further, if you have bad habits, many times, those things come back to bite you.

For example, if you have a habit of going into classes late or going to work late, then you eventually can lose points or get written up. If you chose to do this enough, it could cause you to get a lower grade or to get fired from your job. These are examples of self-sabotage. Your teacher didn't do that to you, nor did your boss. Your actions caused them to make decisions that severely cost you.

It is one thing when someone does something to hurt you. Life happens and some folks aren't nice. On the other hand, it's another thing when you choose to do things to hurt yourself. Another example, you decide to spend money on the latest phone or biggest television and now you don't have enough money to pay rent. This is self-sabotage and doesn't make sense. For this reason, it is important you learn to use discipline and discretion to help yourself succeed. Don't try to be someone else or live up to others "expectations" for you. You get to choose how you want to show up in this life, so just "do you."

As a general rule, don't do things that don't give you some long term benefit. Going in late to work or school, not taking good care of yourself, not investing effort in relationships with your family and friends, being quick-tempered; these are all things that can be considered self-sabotage. You will have enough people trying to keep you down in life without you deciding to lend them a hand.

CONFIDENCE VS ARROGANCE

There is power in demonstrating belief in oneself. It gives others a sense of confidence in you. As you see others have confidence in you, your own confidence will grow. Note that I'm talking about having self-confidence, not being arrogant. There is a difference and people will notice. Notice the difference in how Pharrell and Kanye West communicate with interviewers and you can get an idea of the difference between self-confidence and arrogance.

There will always be hurdles and challenges in your life. Enough of them will come your way without you dragging more of them into your path. Often, it isn't the hurdles or challenges that cause you the most problems, but rather what you do or don't do when or after you have them.

For example, if you get a cut on your arm, realize it is infected, but decide to wait several days before getting it checked out, you leave yourself exposed to severe consequences. Instead of the doctor needing to clean the wound and perhaps put stitches in it, you now could be looking at the possibility of amputation. This is something you had complete control over.

More of us should focus on stopping the things we do to ourselves that work against us. Calling ourselves stupid, being angry with ourselves, punishing ourselves, or depriving ourselves to the extent we don't allow good things to happen to us or we reject them isn't healthy. If we were able to stop doing those things, our lives would be so much richer and easier.

THE POWER OF NEGATIVE THINKING

We all make mistakes and have done things we're not proud of. If we actually feel that way about them, then we should stop doing them or figure out a plan on how to discontinue doing them. Afterward, we need to change our focus to how we can be doing more positive things for ourselves.

Many of us are not reaching our potential because of the significant amount of negative thinking we rehearse in our heads on a daily basis. Negative thinking can often fuel fires, creating damage and destruction in its path.

It can cause you to pull things into your path, or allow others to, that can help destroy you. Take drugs and alcohol, for example. Very rarely does someone try drugs or alcohol for the first time and die or have their health significantly diminished. It does happen, but it's rare. Additionally, rarely does anyone drink and drive and get caught the first time. Nor do most abusive people or bullies suffer severe consequences the first time they do it.

TELLING YOURSELF LIES

No, what happens is they got away with it the first time. This led them to believe they could continue to get away with their behavior without consequences the following times. After that, it was just a new way of living. They made excuses for why they did those things, gained more confidence, got comfortable, and continued to do them. It wasn't until later down the road that their actions caught up with them and caused serious trouble. This is also a form of self-sabotage. In these cases, they did things they knew were wrong but continued until they destroyed themselves and possibly others.

Let's face it; we are all going to die someday. The questions are: How much do you want to sabotage yourself while you are here? What quality of life do you want to have? How much effort are you willing to put into yourself and others to get that quality of life? What sacrifices are you willing to make to get on top?

You can't be the fastest runner in the world, yet drink and party every night, eat fattening foods, and never go to the gym. If you are a fast runner, someone wants to run faster. If you are aiming to make the best grades in your school, someone else wants to be that person as well. You can't get to the top if you are sabotaging yourself by not keeping in shape and not studying.

You need to keep in mind how you may be sabotaging yourself when you do bad things. When you don't eat right, drive drunk or do drugs, what you are sabotaging is your health and potentially the quality of your life and others.

An example of this is texting or drinking while driving. Everyone who texts or drinks while driving doesn't die. Some, who've done it and crashed, probably wish they would have, because now that they've survived, some are wheelchair bound or worse. The quality of their life and perhaps others has been severely diminished by their own actions and there is no going back.

CLIMBING OUT OF HOLES YOU'VE DUG IS HARD WORK

Another example is some of my friends in college who were doing drugs, showing up late to class, flunking out, and getting in trouble with the law. This wasn't someone else hurting them, this was them hurting themselves. They weren't making positive contributions to their own lives. Those are not the types of investments you want to make in yourself. You want to avoid creating problems that either detract from success or that create big holes you need to climb out of. Climbing out of holes takes lots of energy. Further, when you get out of them, you are still going to have to spend more energy catching up. Meaning, if you get strung out on drugs, there is a good chance you can lose your job. If you lose your job, in order to get another one, you will have to clean yourself up. This may mean going to rehab and when you get out, you still have to find a job. By now, you are behind in bills or perhaps have lost your apartment or home. This is what I mean by needing to climb out of a hole you dug and then play catch up.

Simply put, love and care for yourself enough to place value in all of your actions. Don't sabotage yourself by doing things you know you shouldn't be doing because the chances of them catching up with you in one way or another are very high.

Lesson 8.

Don't Fight
The UFC is only on TV

"The only fight you can't lose is the one you don't have."

~ *Unknown*

BE SMART FIRST

Your life is worth defending and fighting for, but 99% of the time my advice is; don't fight. It is much better to talk your way out of a fight, try to compromise, walk away, or run if necessary. When there is a crowd around, backing down, walking away, or running from a fight can be a difficult choice. But don't ever let a crowd persuade you into a fight. On most occasions, even some of the toughest killers; U.S. Military servicemen, martial arts black belts, and Navy Seals, choose to walk away from the vilest insults. They won't fight. They walk unless there is an unavoidable physical threat.

Fighting is not a smart thing and often a poor choice. One can easily win the fight but lose the war; meaning you might beat your opponent, yet, if he or she returns with a gun and shoots you, you've lost the war. One of the toughest men on the planet, Bruce Lee, not just an actor, but a real major fighter, was once asked what he would do if someone pulled a gun on him. He said he would ASK the person what they wanted. He didn't say he'd take the gun. He didn't say he'd kick the guy's butt or any number of other things. Why? Because Mr. Lee understood that while he might have the capability to take the man's gun away, there is always a chance things could go wrong.

I'm not going to get into the rightness or wrongness of the George Zimmerman vs. Trayvon Martin situation, but I want to bring this up because I need you to understand two things. First, assuming you are doing nothing wrong, you can still be a victim of someone with bad intentions. Second, even though you may be protecting yourself, it may get someone killed, which could change the rest of your life. You could wind up being out hundreds of thousands of dollars from trying to protect yourself through our judicial system. There are no winners in that situation, only losers and it is only the degree of loss that may or may not offer any comfort.

Walk Away

Fighting is something that should only be done as a last resort. Often, it makes more sense to walk away from a fight than to engage in one. For example, someone you don't know is teasing you, calling you names while drunk, or being a loud mouth. Why would you want to waste time getting into a confrontation or fight with them? Rule one, know your opponent. This violates that and always increases your risk of things going badly.

You can never look at a person and make the assumption you can beat them. Many a fight has been lost due to underestimating one's opponent and resulted in death. Don't fall into this trap. Fighting is done for one reason; to hurt your opponent. A large number of people are into the MMA and UFC fights that are televised. Some guys and women coming out of those fights are badly hurt, and that is a fight that takes place with a referee and rules!

There are no rules and referees in a street fight. It is you and the other person or in some cases other people if you happen to have that misfortune. With the UFC and MMA fights, it is always one on one. But, in a street fight, often you do not know your opponent, nor do you know the surroundings or the audience. That is three strikes against you before the fighting starts.

I knew a guy name Mike in high school and college who loved to fight. We frequently wound up playing basketball at the same places and he would intentionally pick fights with opposing team members. Mike was very short, thin and didn't look like much of a fighter. His victims would make the mistake of looking at him, sizing him up, and coming to the conclusion they could beat him. They never bothered to examine the audience or their surroundings.

On one particular occasion, there was a guy visiting from Chicago playing on my team. Mistake number one was he thought since he was from Chi-town and playing ball in a "little town like Denver", he didn't have anything to fear. He'd grown up on Chicago's Southside and knew his way around, or so he thought. He was a heck of a ball player and we were beating Mike's team. Mike started running his mouth, as usual, trying to bait the guy into a fight and the guy was falling for it.

I pulled Mr. Chicago guy aside when everyone was discussing a foul. I shared with him that amongst the many people watching us play, were six guys drinking underneath a tree across the way, acting like they weren't paying us any attention. I informed him unless he wanted to fight all of them, he may want to think about his next steps. Very politely, he laughed, thanked me and squashed the conflict with Mike so he could continue to play.

Often there isn't someone around who will pull your coat tail to let you know things aren't as they appear. Too frequently, many people around want to see a good fight and some of those dumb enough to hang around to watch, wind up getting hurt themselves.

This brings me to my next point; don't stand and watch a fight. Walk away. You don't need to be there. If someone starts shooting, you could get hit or trampled as people start to panic and run. If you want to watch one, do so on TV, YouTube, or someplace else far away that's safe. If you choose to watch one up close and personal, son, you too can become a victim. You hear about people all the time who got hurt or killed because they were watching a fight. Don't let this person be you.

Remember, a bullet has no name on it. When people shoot in anger or fear, they are not necessarily thinking straight, which means they are not shooting straight either. They are pointing a deadly weapon in the direction of the person they are angry with and pulling the trigger. This generally leads to chaos and destruction. People start running and trampling each other. You look up and several have severe injuries or could be dead. This is not just talk, it's from personal experience.

I wish everyone would stop right here and take a moment to think about what I just said. There are people in this world we all despise, strongly dislike, or even hate, for that matter. But do we really need to kill them? Is it really worth the very strong possibility of going to prison for ANY amount of time, or for your entire life because you decided to shoot or kill someone?

For example, I stole your car, took your girlfriend, and now you are willing to go to jail or risk the death penalty. You are going to go to jail, where you can't drive your car, even if you got it back and where you can't spend time with your girlfriend, even if you got her back. Really? Don't let your uncontrolled anger or emotional immaturity get you in a situation where you waste years of your life locked up behind bars like an animal. You are better than that.

A TIME TO FIGHT

If you ever do have to fight, then fight to hurt, maim, or worse. As I shared earlier, your life is worth defending. So is the life of someone you care for. Understand that any time you get in a fight you are risking your life or going to jail. Aim to hurt your opponent as quickly as possible. Break him down and disable him. Then get away from wherever you are as soon as possible. Just be prepared to speak with the police, get arrested, go to jail, or if the situation is bad enough, even to trial and maybe prison.

A TIME TO THINK

When you decide to fight, do just that; make it a conscious decision, not a reactive one. Reacting to something without conscious thought can result in consequences that may not be worth it. Think about what those may be, along with the potential risks and how you want to approach the fight.

For example, if someone throws a beer in your face, at that moment, you have hurt pride and you are wet. That's all. On the other hand, if you start fighting, swinging chairs, throwing bottles, or shooting, then there are a number of other issues that may come into play.

Let's say you throw a punch and knock the person out or they fall and hit their head on an object and the person dies. Was it worth it to throw that punch and then potentially go on trial or to jail for assault or murder; all because some stupid drunk threw or spilled beer on you? Remember, you can be absolutely right, but the judicial process can result in an entirely wrong decision. If your punch led to death or paralysis, are you prepared to deal with having either of those two things on your conscience for the rest of your life? Are you willing to pay that knucklehead damages? Was it worth it?

I don't have those answers, but those are things people frequently seem not to think about. Take George Zimmerman, for example. If he'd taken the time to think about the possibility of his current situation happening before he shot Trayvon, do you think he'd have thought all of this was still worth it? I think not. But that's just me guessing. Possibly, he might still think it absolutely was worth the confrontation. Nevertheless, he is going to go through some significant changes in his life because of his actions. This is why I'm asking you to always keep in mind the possible consequences of your actions.

Remember Michael Dunn, the Florida guy who shot into a car full of teenagers, killing Jordan Davis in 2013? Never in his wildest dreams did he think he'd wind up going to jail for what will most likely be the rest of his life. He just had an ax to grind and figured he'd take it out on those young black teens.

Now, let's assume one of those young men actually did pull a gun on him, as he claimed. What if that happened and the judicial system just plain screwed up and got it wrong? How is that helping him now? You see, Mr. Dunn had a choice; he could have pumped his gas and tolerated loud music for a small number of minutes in his life, and then driven off. He could have chosen to drive to another gas station.

Instead, he chose not to. He made a decision to confront the young men. Today, Jordan Davis is dead, and Michael Dunn is in prison because he decided to shoot into a car full of young men he didn't know and were having no real impact on his life. Was it worth it?

Lesson 9.

Character
It's a choice

"It takes 20 years to build a reputation and five minutes to ruin it. If you think about that, you'll do things differently."

~ Warren Buffett

"Parents can only give good advice or put them on the right path, the final forming of a person's character lies in their own hands."

~ Anne Frank

YOUR ACTIONS TELL OTHERS WHO YOU ARE

You can make an enormous difference in the quality of your life by choosing the type of character you want to have. You can be a bum or Agent 007. You can be a medical doctor or a thief. You can be an artist or a pimp. But the reputation you develop for your character will follow you the rest of your life, no matter what profession you choose. Your character will be what your family, friends, and colleagues care about. You get to choose. Think about these with care. This is one of the most important choices you will ever make in life for it is character that defines a man.

If you choose to spend too little time investing in your character, your life will reflect this missed opportunity. As you grow older, people will discuss your character, ethics, values and reputation, often within the same conversations. You want those words to be well-spoken and positive. You should defend your character and reputation as strongly as you'd defend your home or your family. It is that important.

MONEY HAS NOTHING TO DO WITH CHARACTER

If I were to say the only way to make significant money or have a successful career is to have good character, I'd be lying. The movie *The Wolf of Wall Street* will show you that. You can have horrible character and make a ton of money and become financially successful. If you adopt bad character while you may be able to go back, change and rebuild both your character and reputation, you still may never be accepted by some people. It is a thousand times harder to rebuild and rebrand yourself than it is to just build yourself the right way from the start.

Unfortunately, society's values have eroded so much that you don't have to have great talent to make money or have a successful career, depending on how you choose to define "success." Bernie Madoff, who "made off" with billions of dollars of people's money, was financially successful and respected for decades. That is until everyone found out he was a crook. He ruined thousands of people's lives and went to prison at the age of seventy-four. Yes, he had a successful career until his deception and cheating were discovered.

WHAT GOES AROUND COMES AROUND

Some might think, "Hey, that's not a bad trade off. I get to live like a king for thirty or forty years and then go to prison for the rest of my life at age seventy-four. I'd be almost dead at that point anyway." Be that as it may, there is another side of that coin. Both of Bernie's son's lost their jobs and it's doubtful anyone will hire them, at least not for quite some time. Worse, one of his son's committed suicide because of the embarrassment. When you think about the severe stress he placed on his family and his son's suicide, let alone causing thousands of people to suffer financially because of his actions; do you still think that's okay?

Read about Dennis Kozlowski, former CEO of Tyco. In my opinion, when I talk about lacking character, he's a perfect example. Not only did he admittedly spend lavish amounts of corporate money, but he caused people to lose their jobs. If you look at some articles on him from financial magazines, you'll see how everyone raved about how smart he was. He was buying a company every few days. Further, his company was consistently beating Wall Street's expectations.

In 2001, I was consulting and remember listening to all of the accolades and watching him on numerous TV shows for months. He was a hot topic of conversation. I repeatedly told my co-workers he was dirty and it would be just a matter of time before he went to jail. Most laughed at me or blew me off, but I stuck to my convictions.

No, I wasn't a genius. What was crystal clear to me that many people overlooked, was if you are buying a company every few days or once a month, how can you merge their books with yours and keep your accounting straight? It's impossible!

You only have so many employees as part of your merger and acquisition team and, generally speaking, it takes months for the best firms to do only one merger. Yet, he was doing one a week? I don't think so! There are numerous corporate execs that have been lying or cheating over the years and many wound up in prison or suffering the humiliation of being an outcast.

RISKING YOUR REPUTATION FOR PENNIES

I know most of my examples have been executives, but there are everyday people who've risked their reputations for a lot less. They've tried stealing a pack of cigarettes, a toy, clothing, a tool, only to get caught and have a criminal record for something worth as little as a dollar.

A Dallas Cowboy running back, Joseph Randle, who makes over half a million dollars a year, was arrested for stealing one hundred twenty-three dollars of cologne and underwear from a Dillard's department store. Are you kidding me? Now, this guy has a problem. He's either a kleptomaniac and needs help, isn't very bright or both.

He plays for one of the premiere teams in NFL history. A team built on tradition, winning championships and striking fear into their opponents. He makes great money, but he's so caught up in his own world, he failed to connect the negative consequences of his one hundred twenty-three dollar action.

Why anyone would risk their reputation and the possibility of losing their job or getting a decent one in the future for something that is only going to provide short-term gain, is difficult for me to understand. You must keep the big picture in mind all of the time, not just some of the time! If you don't, you too may quickly find out your short-term joy has created significant long-term consequences.

Lesson 10.

Understanding the Game
What to do when trouble comes

"The most important thing to do if you find yourself in a hole is to stop digging."

~ Warren Buffett

CONFRONTING TROUBLE

Sooner or later in life, we all do things that cause us to get into trouble. It may be with a friend, at work, with your family, but it's coming.

In most cases, the best thing to do is openly admit what you did wrong and the sooner, the better. You can tell them you will fix it and if it's fixable, then do so. You must decide, based on the circumstances, which actions are appropriate.

You will not be able to talk your way out of, walk away from, or negotiate every problem you get into. You may even look ridiculously foolish trying, thus, causing you even more embarrassment and loss of credibility. Admitting you made a mistake can be powerful! It disarms your critics and takes away their power. When they try to bring it up, it's not news anymore. Many may look at you and think, "Yeah, he is human, just like the rest of us. Glad he came out and admitted it and I hope he can move on."

Unfortunately, there will always be people who like to see others get chopped down a peg. Some of this is human nature, some is jealousy, and some is hate. You can't control peoples' thoughts or reactions to mistakes, but you can help minimize the damage they can do to you by your actions and having a reputation as a straight shooter.

A TIME TO SHUT UP

Other times, the best thing you can do is keep your mouth shut. Many years ago I got into trouble on my job for doing something I shouldn't have done. It wasn't a legal problem, but rather internal politics and what got me out of trouble was keeping my mouth shut!

I like what a dear friend shared with me. "When you are standing in doo-doo, keep still, because when you start moving around, you just stir up the stink and then everyone smells it." This is very true in that you never want to stir up the mess you are standing in. You want things to calm down quickly, with as few people knowing about it as possible. If you start flinging your arms, shouting, jumping up in down, you might as well just go ahead and plug in a fan along with a neon sign asking everyone to look at you.

Most of the time, the last thing you want when you are in trouble is more attention. Don't talk about it. If you can, downplay it, deny it, and laugh it off. Often you will find you think more people have heard about it than actually have, and fewer people really care. You can create doubt by, not talking about it and continuing to act just like you did before the incident.

When you are in trouble, that's exactly what you want people to have; doubt. If you find yourself in trouble and start doing obvious things like stop speaking, stop dressing nice, start walking with your head held down, then what you are doing is drawing unwanted attention to yourself.

People who may know about your problems are going to look at you and your behavior and think you're guilty because you are acting like it. Others who didn't know about your problem will notice something different about you. They'll either start asking you what is wrong or they'll ask others. You don't want either happening. Your actions, after you get into trouble, can severely help or hinder your real problems. Be very aware of this.

WHEN UNINVITED TROUBLE COMES

Sometimes trouble happens without you doing anything to cause it. You can be in the wrong place at the wrong time. Perhaps some bad kid moves on your block, joins your basketball team, or sits next to you in class and starts picking on you. You had nothing to do with that and did nothing to encourage any of his behavior toward you.

These are more difficult situations to get out of or detect. Generally, when this has happened, I've tried choosing the path of least resistance. This can mean ignoring the person or tolerating them to a degree. At times, when you size a particular situation up, those are not options. You may feel a confrontation is coming and unavoidable. In that case, you need to set boundaries upfront or very quickly. Based on your initial reaction or lack of one, sometimes these kinds of people believe you are weak. You may have to set them straight.

THE IMPORTANCE OF ESTABLISHING BOUNDARIES

This is not a view you may be able to afford for them to have; least you find yourself fighting a bigger battle, possibly even with fists. So, establishing a boundary as soon as you can is important. It may initially cause you some discomfort, but in the long term it can save you from substantially more.

Establishing boundaries can also lead to immediate altercations, but you will need to weigh each incident separately and determine your course of action. Sometimes, you may not be able to avoid conflict. In these cases, preparation and having a course of action planned are your keys to success. You can tell your teacher about another student's bad conduct before you discuss it with that student. You can tell your neighbors you are going to confront a bully and ask for their assistance in doing it. You can notify a police officer about a rowdy fan at a game and let him/her deal with the situation instead of you getting involved. Each of these actions can limit trouble.

ALWAYS FIND OUT THE RULES

One of the best pieces of advice I can give you is to know the rules of any game before you play. This doesn't mean just the "standard" ones but the "unspoken" ones too. Knowing your teacher's, coach's, or even your boss's pet peeves can mean all the difference in the world to your success. For example; let's say a coach or teacher gets infuriated when players or students are late for practice or class. Now you show up late. Rest assured, it's going to be much harder for you to get solid playing time or good grades. They may have a tendency to be significantly more critical about your ability to play or about the answers on your homework or exams. These are "must knows" for you.

I once had a manager who was always riding me about everything. She'd pick out the tiniest mistakes on bills I processed. She'd critique my comments in meetings, and tell me I should have had my work done sooner, even when it was completed ahead of schedule. No matter how good it was, she still had a negative comment.

I was sharing my frustrations with a co-worker one day and they told me that I was frequently a few minutes late to work. I told them while that was true sometimes, I was only a few minutes late and I always stayed late to make up for it.

They told me all my manager cared about was who was in their seat working by eight o'clock in the morning. She did a walk by every day and would make notes of who was sitting and working and who wasn't. If you showed up on her list more than a few times, even if you were only a minute or two late, you were "on her list."

For the next several weeks, I committed myself to being into work before eight o'clock. Sure enough, her attitude and disposition toward me significantly changed. It's amazing what coming in only four or five minutes earlier did to my evaluation and our relationship. Was it silly? Yes, from my point of view, but I needed a paycheck and a raise. Bucking her system and continuing to get in trouble for it, when all she was asking me to do was come in on time wasn't worth the hassle.

Once I started coming in on time, whether or not I did anything of significance for the rest of the day didn't matter, but being on time did. That was "her thing." Had I been more aware of that earlier, I could have saved myself some grief. She would never have conversations with anyone about her expectation. This is exactly why I call these unspoken rules. It is important to find out what makes people tick and identify those unspoken rules they may use to judge you, especially when they are your manager, coach or teacher.

Lesson 11.

When I Become an Adult, I Can Do Anything I Want!
The hard reality check

"Men do not quit playing because they grow old; they grow old because they quit playing."

~ *Oliver Wendell Holmes Jr.*

"When I was a child, I couldn't wait to become an adult because I knew being an adult would mean everyone would act mature and there wouldn't be any more game playing or dealing with childish people. Man, was I ever wrong!"

~ *David Dixon*

THE MYTH

LOL! This is truly one of the BIGGEST myths young people believe. I believed it and so did every other kid on my block! Man, if only that were even half true, your dad would be happy! This is the opposite view of adults who say children have life so easy. Yet, as young children, and even older ones, you have so little control. You are told what to wear, what to do, and when to be where. You're also told when to eat, bathe and study. I remember when I was a child and teen and I found that frustrating.

One of the biggest disappointments I had when I first came into adulthood was realizing even though I was out from underneath my parents, I STILL couldn't do whatever I wanted, whenever I wanted. During my first week as a freshman in college, all of the new students were hanging out and it got to be midnight. Some started saying they needed to go or they'd be in trouble. When questioned, they replied they'd get in trouble for missing curfew. Then it dawned on them we didn't have a curfew in college. So, up and out we stayed until two, three, four o'clock in the morning.

The problem was, after two or three nights of partying and still needing to get to class at 8:00 am, we were dog tired and falling asleep in class. It was at this point most of us came to the realization there was a reason why only the freshmen were up and out most of the night. The older classmen knew what we had to learn; you can't function very well the next day without sleep, let alone stay up and get all of that homework done the next evening.

THE PERILS OF NOT ACCEPTING RESPONSIBILITY

Attending college was the beginning of adulthood and a harsh reality check. It's when, whether you consciously become aware of it or not, you start making adult choices. Some classmates continued to hang out into the wee hours of the night, long after the majority of us stopped. Many of them soon dropped out or were kicked out because they weren't making the grade. There were no parents around to tell us to go to bed. Those unable to figure it out quickly were the ones flunking or dropping out before the end of the first semester.

I remember becoming an adult, getting a job, and coming to the realization that I now had a surrogate parent; my boss! Now I had to come to work at a particular time, perform at a certain standard, and out-work my peers in order to get promoted. I also had to pay my bills and rent on time.

Yes, I was grown, but I still couldn't do whatever I wanted. In my "free time" I had to do laundry, clean my apartment, study, see my girlfriend, and on and on it went. I realized it was never going to end. I was always going to have to be accountable to someone or to do something.

YOU WILL ALWAYS BE ACCOUNTABLE TO SOMEONE

Even if you are a CEO, you are accountable to your stockholders, Board of Directors, and employees. When the company you run makes mistakes, people lose jobs and shareholders lose money. Look at the company Blackberry; from the end of the 1990's to the early 2000's, they made one of the most popular mobile phones in the world. But how many of your friends own one today or even know what a Blackberry is? Things change.

Musicians must have listeners. If they stop putting out great music, they lose their fans. Occasionally, even if they continue putting out great music, their fans gets tired of their sound anyway and they still lose them. It happens, but you have to keep trying to put out good products, messages, music, and materials. If not, you too can find yourself displaced or replaced by someone doing a better job at what you do than you.

Theoretically, you do have the choice of doing anything you want, but as I've shared, there are always consequences. For every action, there is a reaction that can be good or bad. You are responsible for getting what you want. If you want to be LeBron James, you're going to have to practice hard and consistently. If you want to be a famous actor like Denzel Washington, you're going to have to practice hard and consistently. If you want to be a phenomenally powerful and smart /CEO like Steve Jobs or Kenneth I. Chenault, you are going to have to work long hours and be able to consistently grow revenue. You'll need to have the patience to experience numerous failures and the smarts to surround yourself with other very sharp people with big dreams.

Understand whatever you do, in order to be successful or excellent at it, you're going to have to put in a substantial amount of work and you will be held accountable to someone. If you are allergic to either, money will probably be allergic to your pocket! Being able to "do anything you want" is an illusion based on severe misconception.

A TIME TO BE SELFISH

There is one important thing you can do as an adult to help make your life easier and that is find something you really enjoy doing, then pursue it and do it well. Don't let the fear of losing people keep you from pursuing your dreams. They are your dreams, not your friend's or your parent's dreams.

Have you ever given a friend some help? Perhaps you've helped them complete a term paper, assisted them with yard work, or even some personal issue? Then, a while later, you need assistance, but they are too busy, won't return your calls/texts, or they tell you no. Now you know they are a user.

Well, first, congratulations on finding out they may not be as good of a friend as you thought. Better to find out now rather than later when you have more important needs. The hard truth is, very few people will be there for you when you need assistance.

Sometimes it is important that you are selfish with your time. If getting your car running is a priority for you, then you can't spend time trying to help someone else get theirs running. Getting your car running should be your first priority because it is definitely their option.

Navigating through adulthood absolutely has its challenges, but pursuing excellence is a sure way to take care of yourself and minimize dependency on others. You don't have to wait to be an adult to adopt this attitude either. You can start right now. It will allow you to build your future on solid ground, hopefully doing something you enjoy. It can give you freedom in that you are working on something that may not feel like work. Every person born has a talent or skill, but it is up to each of us to find out what that is and then use it to our advantage.

When you do something you love, you create "good" energy and that energy is what sustains you and helps push you. It is also what others feel and attracts them to you.

NAVIGATING THROUGH LIFE

Often in life, you will have to navigate through weeds to get to greatness. What this means is sometimes there are metaphoric weeds in your way that you must cut down in order to get to your particular path. Other times, when you see weeds or obstacles in your path, you don't need to cut them or move them, you need to go around them. Everything doesn't have to be difficult. Sometimes there are easier choices than hacking through weeds and picking up and moving heavy obstacles out of your way.

A good example is not getting along with schoolmates or people at your job. Sometimes you spend significant effort trying to change those relationships when instead you need to change your environment. You may need to switch schools or change jobs. If you've tried this and have the same problems at different schools or jobs, then perhaps you should do more extensive self-evaluation. The common denominator here is "you." Sometimes you really are the problem, not the schools, not the teachers, not your schoolmates, and not your job or manager. Sometimes you need to take a hard look at yourself and figure out what it is you are doing that is getting in the way of your success. Once you can identify and correct that, you will soar!

Lesson 12.

Sagging Pants
It's about your mind, stupid!

"There are only two races on this planet-the intelligent and the stupid."

~ *John Fowles*

"If we demonstrate an inability to commit the simplest of tasks, like pulling up our pants, then what does that communicate to anyone we run across? What real woman would honestly want a man who can't even pull up his damn pants?

~ *David Dixon*

THE ERA OF STUPIDITY

I debated long and hard about putting my thoughts on sagging pants into this book, but my duty as your father and as a man overcame me. The bottom line is this; I don't give a damn if everyone else is "saggin", don't you do it! This is one of the most disturbing things I've seen young and grown men do and they don't even get how pathetically sad it is!

Sagging pants comes from prisons. Sometimes gay guys would use it to advertize their sexual availability. Other times and more common, men would go into prison wearing belts, but the belts would be confiscated to keep them from being used as weapons or as a means to hang either themselves or other inmates. For this reason, either their pants wouldn't stay up without a belt and would sag or inmates would lose weight and their pants would sag. So, they had no choice but to let them. This may be fine in prison, but since when did it become "mainstream" to adopt styles from those who couldn't stay in it?

This is the sign of a fool.

If a man can't pull up his pants, what can he do? Why would any real man want to emasculate himself to this degree? That is what we do as men and young men when we demonstrate to the world an inability to pull up our own pants. It's insulting to others and you'd think it would be insulting to us, as men, to give the impression we can't figure out how to pull up our pants.

MALE REGRESSION

Without stating it, on a deeper level, when we sag our pants; we look like we need help pulling them up. The only thing missing is for us to start walking around with pacifiers in our mouths! Our parents didn't raise us to grow up to be babies or dress like fools!

As a society, what does this say about its expectations of its men? It shows and demonstrates laziness. A society that creates an environment allowing grown men to walk down the street with their damn underwear showing doesn't speak much for hope, strength, or character. But rather, it speaks to a society of indifference, tolerance of foolishness, and disrespect towards its women.

Are these the type of men we want to put faith in to fight for our country? Raise our children? Represent our country at the Olympics? Represent us in court? "Hi your Honor, I'm here to represent David Dixon in his capital murder trial, but I haven't figured out how to pull up my pants." Is this the type of attorney we want to hire to help keep us out of jail or keep us from the death penalty?

Doubtful.

One of the first things we learned as a child was how to get dressed. The only thing we, as teenagers and grown men, exhibit when we sag our pants, is that we are in a state of regression. We represent a new portion of society with a sagging mind; a part of society who "society is okay with" because it has low or no expectations for us. While some of us are focusing on exactly how low our pants can go, the elite of society are focusing their children's attention on how high their grades can be. They are encouraging their children to focus on how high they can climb the corporate ladder, how big they can grow their own businesses, and how high of a political office they can obtain. Do you see the stark contrast?

DRESSING FOR DIS-RESPECT

Sagging pants goes even deeper. The apparent lack of self-esteem that would allow us to walk around with our pants pulled down, drifts into other areas of our life and our mind. First, it's just the pants, but then, if we don't have our pants pulled up, why bother combing our hair or brushing our teeth? Why look for a job today when we can look for one tomorrow instead? Why not get into a fight, it's not like we're dressed sharp anyway? And what difference does it make? People don't expect anything of us and don't treat us with respect anyway.

Sagging pants is the beginning of a slippery slope that has significant potential to slide entire lives downward. Even if we are at the rock bottom of society; have lost a job, just got out of prison, how does sagging our pants contribute to lifting up our spirit or bettering our current situation? It doesn't. Instead, it negatively impacts our self-perception and worse, others perceptions of us.

Does anyone you know who is trying to climb the ladder of success, sag his pants?

CREATING A "VICTIM" MENTALITY

It shows a sense of immature rebelliousness against social norms for all of the wrong reasons. It's blatantly disrespectful to women and conveys a message of inability in spite of our actual ability.

Have you ever seen a guy or woman who's dressed to the "nines" and then you get up close to them and they don't smell fresh? You were surprised and wonder how that could be, right? How can this person dress so sharp and yet stink? This is what happens with sagging pants but only in the reverse. People see us and wonder what is wrong before they even get to know us for who we truly are.

When a woman looks at us and turns away in disgust, we can label her as "thinking she's too good." In our minds, we can twist things around to tell ourselves that she is the one with the problem. Later on, "she" can become "they", as in all of those women. This can easily translate into "all of those white people" or "all of those black people" or all of those "rich people." Sagging our pants puts us in a position to be on the outside of society, looking at those on the inside with disdain, disrespect, callousness, or even hatred in our eyes. It establishes an opportunity for us to mistakenly take the position that "we're okay and everyone else isn't."

CREATING LASTING IMAGES

It's true; we never get a second chance to make a first impression. What do we want someone's first impression of us to be? More of us should think about that before we make the choice to step out of our homes with our pants sagging and underwear showing. Do we really want to embed in anyone's mind; their first impression of us is that of a guy who can't even pull up his pants? Or worse, a guy who has one of his main points of focus directed on sagging his pants just right, so they go below his butt cheeks in order to show off his matched or mismatched underwear? What kind of fool does this? Is this really the first impression we want to give a young lady we are interested in as a potential girlfriend?

How do we overcome this image we've placed in her mind? It's almost like seeing some guy spitting in a woman's face in a nightclub and the next thing you know he's sitting in your office interviewing for a job. It won't matter how articulate he is. It won't matter how many degrees or certifications he has. Nor will it matter how well-dressed and mannerly he is, or even how often he smiles because you still have that image embedded in your mind of him spitting in a woman's face. Is it worth it to potentially leave anyone with either of those impressions?

Why bother having to overcome that image when we can simply keep our pants pulled up like they were intended to be from the beginning? This is putting obstacles in our path and then trying to maneuver around them. We don't need to do that. We'll find that life has more than enough obstacles without us adding to them.

Even the most foolish individual can be taken quite seriously if he is dressed well and says nothing that offends. A little time spent on clothing, grooming, and being quiet can get us half way to our goal.

Everyone needs to understand when we die, what we've left is really a reflection of who we are, frozen in time. The memories, images, photographs, videos and writings, reflect our body of work we did while we were here.

Let's keep our pants pulled up!

Lesson 13.

Judgment, Drive, Passion, and Perseverance

Don't leave home without them

"The closer you get to excellence in your life, the more friends you'll lose. People love you when you are average because it makes them comfortable. But when you pursue greatness, it makes them uncomfortable. Be prepared to lose some people on your journey."

~ Tony A. Gaskins, Jr.

STARTING A SUCCESSFUL LIFE

There are four critical things that will help you succeed in life; they are drive, passion, perseverance, and sound judgment. The blend of these four can almost be a super power for you.

Whatever you do, find something that drives you, that you are passionate about, and that you are willing to do over and over again through tough times. You can be driven, but if you do not use sound judgment, you will fail. You can be passionate, but not have perseverance, and you will fail. There are several other combinations, but you get my point. All four together are the requirements for success.

I've had many difficult times in life. I've lost my grandmother and uncle who I loved dearly and depended on emotionally. I've been fired from a job, struggled with relationships, and was hospitalized with a staph infection that almost took the lower half of my left leg. When I was in high school, my stepfather passed away three weeks after marrying your grandmother. By the time I'd completed my undergrad degree, I'd gone to fifteen schools in five different states. These are only a few challenging experiences, but I'm sharing them because, without judgment, drive, passion, and perseverance tied to faith, there is no way I'd have made it.

In life, you will fall down and you will get knocked down, but it is your level of judgment, drive, passion and perseverance that will pick you back up. Without them, you will tend to stay down. In life, you will run into people who will try to knock you down either emotionally or physically. Some will be cruel and when they see you are down, they will think they have beaten you and even go so far as to rejoice in your pain and sorrow.

Other people may try to manipulate your mind by telling you that you'll never make it without them and try to convince you that you need them. When you leave anyway, they may curse you and swear at you, telling you that you'll never amount to anything without them.

THE "NAY" SAYERS

I refer to these types of people as part of the "crabs in a bucket" crew. This refers to people who don't want you to succeed and if you get close, they'll reach up and try to pull you back down. Don't believe them. No one person holds all of the keys that contribute to your success! Should you run across these types of cruel, damaging, or negative people; ease away from them. You don't need to listen to them or believe them because they have obviously underestimated your abilities.

In a corporation, some might be able to keep you from rising up in a particular organization or company. If so, transfer to a different organization or find a job with a different company. There are plenty of other companies out there. Even better, there are plenty of other people you can choose as friends who can help you.

In music, someone may try to keep you from selling a song to a group of producers because you won't write it or sing it the way they want you to. Try again somewhere else or produce it yourself.

In sports, you can be on a team where the coach is a problem. Move on. Change schools or teams if you must. Just continue to do your best.

In each of these examples, perhaps, they may want you to do something for them you are unwilling to do. Regardless of their reasons, don't let them get inside your head and destroy your drive, your gift, your energy, or your power! At the end of the day, they are just another person like you! Perhaps you can learn useful lessons or bad examples from them that will benefit you. Just ensure you keep going and don't get stuck in a battle with them. You may have to suffer through the process as you plan your next moves, but this is common. Keep moving!

OVERCOMING ADVERSITY AND CHALLENGES

When I was a non-management employee for a major phone company, I didn't have my college degree yet and I had a supervisor who told me I wasn't management material. When I pressed her for more insight, she stated I had no managerial skills that she could see. It hurt. I was disappointed and frustrated because I'd been busting my behind trying to do great work. I volunteering for team committees, worked overtime, and always assisted my peers, with hopes I'd be recognized and able to move into a management position. All I wanted to do was take a management test and let that test determine if I had the skills for the job I wanted. I went to her manager as well as to the district manager to express my frustration, but they all supported her and said I couldn't take the test. I went as far as to ask what the purpose was of having a test that was supposedly developed to determine your skill level if they were going to determine it instead?

Nevertheless, I didn't give up and I was able to move under a different supervisor. Unfortunately, this supervisor wasn't helpful either. In fact, she didn't like me and was doing her best to fire me. But God is good. This second supervisor was so anxious to fire me; she decided I needed to be put on a very difficult and boring project.

Fortunately for me, unbeknown to her at the time, that project afforded me the opportunity to work with several different types of software and gave me more exposure to people outside of our organization. This helped me to significantly grow my skill set and my value. Within a few months, I had a few vice presidents of the company flying in to see the work I was doing.

When she found out, she made every attempt she could to pull me back into doing the work I'd been doing previously. Thankfully, my new manager for the large project had our district manager's ear and they decided I'd stay working on the larger project full-time. I continued to flourish, which positioned me to get promoted into management. My smile was barely containable.

OUTSMARTING YOUR DETRACTORS

What were the keys to success here? First, my judgment; I decided not to get an attitude with either of the supervisors who were not helping me. I also didn't argue with them when they angered me. Don't get me wrong, I wanted to. I was aware that I needed to protect my reputation throughout the company and any negative behavior on my part would put that at risk. Angering those supervisors would only have resulted in them talking negatively about me to other managers. For this reason, I had to eat my anger and keep acting like a professional. I also looked for other opportunities outside of the company, but quickly came to understand that without a college degree, it wasn't going to be easy for me to explore other options paying as well.

Second, loaded with the above information, I realized I needed to pursue completion of my college degree with a stronger sense of urgency so I would have the credentials to back up my intelligence.

Third, I continued to develop my skill set at work. I continued to learn the new software I was exposed to and I took on learning process, program and project management. I also volunteered to lead one of the new process improvement teams. However, because I did such a good job with that one, I was given two additional teams to lead.

Several of my peers had the same opportunity to lead process improvement teams, but they didn't want to because they felt they were being asked to do more than they were getting paid for. They also teased me about doing it and told me I was getting used. They were right. Management was using me to an extent. But I was using them too because I was continuing to develop and gain more skills. This made me marketable and more valuable to them.

Finally, I excelled at leading these teams and my reputation not only got better, but it afforded me the opportunity to work with more supportive managers. Along the way, I finished my degree. All of this led to interviews for management positions, which I got. It took about three years, but I accomplished my goal.

Lesson 14.

Define What's Important

What are you doing and why are you doing it?

"The battle you are going through is not fueled by the words or actions of others; it is fueled by the mind that gives it importance."
~ Shannon L. Alder

PAINTING THE PICTURE YOU WANT

Look at what you are doing in your life and why you are doing it. Is it for your own ego? Does what you are doing add any value to you, your life, your family, or your others? Is it self-destructive? These are tough questions you'll want to ask yourself before you start doing the wrong things.

Take the time to write down things that are important to you and the benefits. If the benefits aren't there, stop doing them and change your focus. So many people are lost in life because they don't have a plan or they follow other people's plans.

There are some things you must do. You may be required to please your parents, teachers, friends or family. But sometimes, when the things being asked of you are not emotionally or physically healthy, you need to do a "gut check." Take the time to think about why you feel it is necessary to do them or why they are asking you to. Do your own cost/benefits analysis. Ask yourself what will it cost you and what is the benefit to you or them. When the cost exceeds the benefit then either; don't do it, stop doing it or work on an exit strategy.

UNDERSTANDING YOUR OWN JOURNEY

Many times in life, you may find yourself in situations where you feel it is necessary to do things based on your family, friends or co-workers wishes. You may want to be liked, fit in, or be respected. For example, I know of a family who favored one son over the other because he was a math major. The other son felt he had to become a math major also in order to get their affection and attention. Sad isn't it? It was sad for the parents and the children.

The real questions here are; does math really interest you? Is it something you can put your heart and soul into and enjoy doing it? If not, reconsider following that path. It may be difficult to understand this but if your parents or friends aren't giving you the love you feel you deserve, changing yourself into something you are not, isn't going to help. At least not for the long term. I don't believe you can ever make someone love you. It has to be their choice. If they can only give you conditional love, then you need to recognize that isn't love. That is control or manipulation. There is a difference.

I'm not stating this to suggest you disobey your parents or don't make efforts to do the things they ask. Rather, what I'm suggesting is that you find your comfort zone and do those things that are going to have a positive impact on your life. Think about the big picture.

BE THE BEST YOU THAT YOU CAN BE

You should adopt a mentality that you deserve the best you can make of yourself. If you put that work in, good things will come to you and happen for you. It's like Karma. Look back over your life at some of your schoolmates and older people you've admired.

Now, also take a look at the past three to five years of your friend's lives. Ask yourself; what were they doing then and what are they doing now? What differences do you see? Do you still think of them with the same level of respect? Have they changed for the better or worse? Have they grown? Are there things they are doing that if you did, it would help you?

Now look at yourself. How far have you come in the past three years? How have you matured? What are you doing better or worse and why? Get those answers clear for yourself and then sufficiently focus on correcting your behavior so you eliminate the bad things you've been doing and extend the good ones.

THE IMPORTANCE OF REFLECTION

Every year, you should get in the habit of reflecting on what you've done and how you've improved. If you have not seen the improvements you want, ask why? Sometimes there are valid reasons. Major events like; death, a loss of a parent's job, illness, a major natural catastrophe, etc., these types of things can happen and interfere with your ability to grow as you desired.

Even through painful situations you can still grow. You may grow in faith, patience, and understanding of how to deal with difficult situations and challenges. You may also gain valuable knowledge. Do this same evaluation of your friends as well. Sometimes, it is time to move on and get the wrong people out of your life and the right people in.

Notes to Parents

"It doesn't matter who my father was; it matters who I remember he was."

~ *Anne Sexton*

"Having a child and choosing to walk away is one of the most despicable things a man can do."

~ *David A. Dixon*

Dear Parents,

TIME AND TRUTH

In talking with several young men and women from various high schools, as well as friends and other parents, it turns out that what our children mainly want from us is our time. They also want us to be honest and forthcoming.

Many of us have smoked marijuana, used alcohol, and other drugs. We absolutely do not want our children doing these and other things we may have done.

Lying to them about our past usually doesn't do them any good. If anything, it can build mistrust and give them excuses to make bad decisions. When we are asked about our experiences, at the appropriate age and believe me, that's probably around ages 9 or 10 for many of our children, being truthful is the best choice. Also, when we tell the truth, we never have to remember which lie we told later.

Remember some of the crass comments made in our classes, on our bus, and in our neighborhood or school by some of the children when we were ten years old? Many of us weren't as naïve as our parents thought we were at that age!

It's imperative for us as parents to understand our young children are honestly not as naïve, sheltered, or dumb as we may want to believe. The Internet has bombarded them with information and images that hit them all the time. Even television is much less censored than it used to be, let alone the radio. If you don't think so, just listen to the lyrics of some of the songs on the radio. If you don't think they "comprehend" what those lyrics mean, ask them. I guarantee you most of the time they know exactly what the lyrics are referring to. If the lyrics are talking about sex and drugs, while our child may not be doing either, they do understand the topics.

ACTIVE FATHERHOOD

Fathers and men, our children need male role models. Our actions speak 10,000 times louder than any of our words. If we don't take the time to be the men they need to see, there are numerous other young and grown men with less moral fortitude who will be the examples they can choose to mirror. Who can raise our child better than us and with more dedication than us? If we decide to relinquish that responsibility to someone else and our children wind up with poor grades, in trouble with the law, or strung out on drugs, then that is on us. How much guilt will we have? How do we resolve that in our mind?

These are our children, regardless of the circumstances that brought them into this world. They didn't ask to be here. We owe it to ourselves and more importantly to them to be there to direct their lives to the best of our ability. Some of us may not be the greatest dads, but we can learn to be better ones by watching our friends, co-workers, colleagues, and neighbors. We can mimic good behavior and have candid conversations with each other. We must also be willing to let others take the lead. We can read, attend support groups, and most certainly, we can ask other fathers!

Many of us are battling the same challenges; no money, prison records, bad relationships with our children's mothers, no jobs, but some of us are still being attentive and involved fathers. Don't buy into the "quality time" excuse. Quality time only happens as a small slice of the quantity of time we put in. If you've ever been in the room with a sick child, you may not be providing their medical attention, but just the fact you are there with them speaks volumes.

There are a number of positive choices we can each make to stay active in our children's lives. These choices start with not allowing our own behavior to be different from our words. Frankly, this will require that some of us grow up and mature. We can't tell them all of the horror stories about drinking and driving when they see us doing it and successfully coming home every day. They'll think if we're doing it and are fine, they will be fine too. If this is you, surely death and destruction are following you. Do we want our children to face that? They trust us and our actions do speak louder than our words. If we're doing drugs, drinking and telling them not to, they can't hear a word we are saying because our silent actions are screaming so loudly.

DEALING WITH YOUR CHILDREN'S MOTHER

Many of us, including me, have ex-wives. Dealing with them when it comes to our children can be difficult. This doesn't excuse us from finding ways to minimize conflict and build a partner relationship. This is all about the children, it's not about them. Everything doesn't have to be a discussion or an argument. We can limit our conversations with them to only being about the children. There are too many different situations to get into this in detail within the context of this book, but I want us to encourage each other to stay as active as we can in our children's lives. It is simply too dangerous for our sons and daughters not to go all in.

TOO NICE

If you're a mother raising your son, I want to encourage you to follow through on your words regarding discipline. Boys and young men are usually hard-headed. My mom wasn't much of a yeller but when she did get to that point, my brother and I knew we'd really screwed up and spankings were usually on the way. She always meant what she said. When she told us she wasn't going to ask us again to; clean up our rooms, take out the trash or clean the kitchen, she meant exactly just that. There was no rescue from dad, grandma, or anybody else who might be around. We were done and on punishment. If we talked back, the punishments got extended.

Being nurturing and mothering to our children is good, but only to a degree. Our children are going to grow up and hopefully be able to make it on their own with the right guidance. Our boys are going to grow up, have girlfriends, wives, and families of their own they will need to provide for and take care of. It becomes more challenging for them to do this when they didn't learn to be; responsible, dependable, respectful, consistent, and self-sufficient at home. It also makes it more difficult if they don't learn consequences for their behavior at home. In the real world, they won't get a paycheck if they don't show up for work and their lights won't stay on if they don't pay the bill. If we don't hold them accountable for their actions in the home, we are creating an unrealistic environment for them because the real world will hold them accountable.

When a young man grows up and leaves the house, he should not be looking for another mother! When it's the right time, he should be looking for a mate and be capable of performing basic partner skills like; cooking, ironing, laundry, and cleaning. Knowing how to do other things like mowing the lawn, painting a wall, and replacing the parts inside of a toilet are an added bonus. If you are a dad or mom and don't know how to do some of these things, it's okay. Ask one of your friends to teach him. There is nothing wrong with seeking help.

BABY BOY

I have a friend who was eighteen years old and his mother still cooked, washed, and ironed his clothes for him. That was sad to observe. It was sad that she was willing to do it and sadder that he was willing to let her. His mother, probably without consciously knowing it, was sending him to another woman, with no skills to take care of his basic needs, let alone hers.

FOUNDATION

Young adults also need a foundation. They need something they can come back to if they go out and get lost in the world. It is our job to provide that for them. Several high school students shared with me that what they needed from their parents was: spiritual guidance, advice, affirmation, values, and intimacy.

They want spiritual guidance because when their road gets tough, they want something to believe in and lean on so they don't give up on life. They want advice, not because they will always use it, but they hear it and it helps them develop their own minds and thoughts. They want affirmation because it lets them know someone cares about them and they are on the right path. They want you to show them values because it helps them form their own. It gives them something to look at in terms of defining what success is and isn't. They also want intimacy; to be hugged and kissed. Most of us do and if we don't, in too many cases it is either because we weren't raised with hugs and kisses or we were abused by someone who took advantage of our innocence.

Being an adult is tough. Being a parent is even tougher. But in some instances, we may be all our children feel they have. They may struggle in school, with friendships or other things, but knowing they have us can make the difference between life or death.

LEARNING FROM OUR CHILDREN

One thing I've learned as a parent is that we should not be afraid or feel insecure about learning from our children. As they get older, it often becomes a two-way street; they learn a lot from us and we learn a little from them. Just as they must continue to grow as children, we must continue to grow as parents and adults. The saying "when you know better, you do better," should be true for us and our children.

The Higher, The Fewer,
David

P.S.

The closing, "The Higher, The Fewer", is something I adopted from a good friend, Joe Jones. It basically means, the higher you climb in life, the fewer people will be in that circle. Whether this relates to climbing the corporate ladder, via job title, spirituality, etc., the fewer people will be willing, interested or able to get to that level. – David

About The Author

David A. Dixon is a graduate of Mercer University in Atlanta, Georgia, where he received a Bachelor's Degree in Business Administration. After 15 years in the telecommunications industry, he decided to pursue a writing career. This is his second published book. His first published book was *Notes to My Daughter*. A third book, a novel, *Pivotal Moments*, will be released later this year. A fourth book, *CHAOS!* is set to be released in 2016. Dixon currently resides in the Metropolitan Denver area.

Sources:

1. http://healthmovejoy.blogspot.com/2013/07/learning-to-walk.html

"The two most important days in your ..,
http://www.goodreads.com/quotes/505050 - Mark Twain-the-two-most-important-days-in-your-life-are-the (accessed October 24, 2014).

"The road to success is dotted with many tempting parking ..,
http://www.goodreads.com/quotes/287461 - Will Rogers-the-road-to-success-is-dotted-with-many-tempting-parking (accessed October 24, 2014).

"The higher mental development of woman, the less possible...,
http://Brainyquote.com/words/co/congenial146985.html - Emma Goldman-the-higher-mental-development-of-woman-the-less-possible (accessed October 24, 1014)

"Conservatives say teaching sex education in the public...,
http://izquiotes.com/quote/300517 - Beverly Mickens-conservatives-say-teaching-sex-education-in-the-public (accessed October 24, 2014)

"The worst lies are the lies we tell ourselves...,
http://www.goodreads.com/quotes/434284-the-worst-lies-are-the-lies-we-tell-ourselves-we - Richard Bach-the-worst-lies-are-the-lies- (accessed February 28, 2015)

"The only fight you can't lose is the one...,
http://www.searchquotes.com/quotation/The_only_fight_you_can%27t_lose_is_the_one_you_don%27t_have/508512/ (accessed October 24, 2014)

"It takes 20 years to build a reputation and five...,
http://www.brainyquote.com/quotes/quotes/w/warrenbuff108887.html - Warren Buffett-it-takes-20-years-to-build-a-reputation-and-five (accessed October 24, 2014)

Sources: (cont'd)

"Parents can only give good advice or put them on the...,
http://www.brainyquote.com/quotes/quotes/a/annefrank120963.html
-parents-can-only-give-good-advice-or-put-them-on-the (accessed
October 24, 2014)

"The most important thing to do if you find yourself...,
http://www.goodreads.com/quotes/9095-the-most-important-thing-
to-do-if-you-find-yourself Warren Buffet-the-most-important-thing-
to-do-if-you-find-yourself (accessed October 24, 2014)

"Men do not quit playing because they grow old...,
http://www.brainyquote.com/quotes/quotes/o/oliverwend103915.htm
l - Oliver Wendell Holmes-men-do-not-quit-playing-because-they-
grow-old (accessed October 24, 2014)

"There are only two races on this planet – the intelligent...,
http://izquotes.com/quote/229599 - John Fowles-there-are-only-two-
races (accessed October 24, 2014)

"The closer you get to excellence in life, the more friends you'll
lose...,
http://www.tumblr.com/search/tony+a+gaskins+jr
(accessed October 24, 2014)

"The battle you are going through is not fueled by the words or
actions...,
http://www.goodreads.com/quotes/1285441-the-battle-you-are-
going-through-is-not-fueled-by - Shannon L. Alder
(accessed October 24, 2014)

"It doesn't matter who my father was: it matters who I...,
http://www.goodreads.com/quotes/search?utf8=%E2%9C%93&q=%
E2%80%9CIt+doesn%27t+matter+who+my+father+was%3B+it+m
atters+who+I+remember+he+was.%E2%80%9D+&commit=Search
– Anne Sexton
(accessed October 24, 2014)

www.ingramcontent.com/pod-product-compliance
Lightning Source LLC
Chambersburg PA
CBHW060323070426
42446CB00049B/2010